Contents

Back to School 1

Theme 1 **Off to Adventure!**
Selection Connections 9
Cliff Hanger 11
Reading-Writing Workshop:
   A Personal Narrative 26
The Ballad of Mulan 31
The Lost and Found 47
Monitoring Student Progress 62
   Connecting and Comparing Literature . . . 62
   Preparing for Tests 66

Focus on Poetry 77

Theme 2 **Celebrating Traditions**
Selection Connections 93
The Keeping Quilt 95
Reading-Writing Workshop:
   Instructions 110
Grandma's Records 115
The Talking Cloth 130
Dancing Rainbows 145
Monitoring Student Progress 161
   Connecting and Comparing Literature . . . 161
   Preparing for Tests 165

Focus on Trickster Tales 177

Contents

Theme 3   **Incredible Stories**

Selection Connections 193

Dogzilla 195

Reading-Writing Workshop:

   A Story 210

The Mysterious Giant of Barletta 215

Raising Dragons 230

The Garden of Abdul Gasazi 245

Monitoring Student Progress 261

   Connecting and Comparing Literature . . . 261

   Preparing for Tests 265

Student Handbook 277

   Spelling 279

     How to Study a Word

     Words Often Misspelled

     Take-Home Word Lists

   Grammar and Usage: Problem Words . . 295

   Proofreading Checklist 296

   Proofreading Marks 297

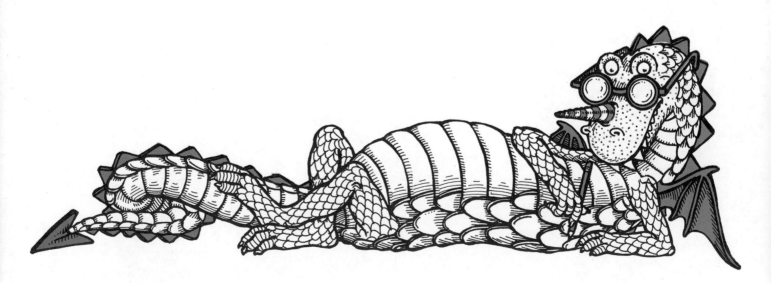

Name _____

Strategy Workshop

As you listen to the story "The Rule," by Anne Cameron, you will stop from time to time to do some activities on these practice pages. These activities will help you think about different strategies that can help you read better. After completing each activity, you will discuss what you've written with your classmates and talk about how to use these strategies.

Remember, strategies can help you become a better reader. Good readers

- use strategies whenever they read

- use different strategies before, during, and after reading

- think about how strategies will help them

Name _____

Strategy 1: Predict/Infer

Use this strategy before and during reading to help make predictions about what happens next or what you're going to learn.

Here's how to use the Predict/Infer strategy:

1. Think about the title, the illustrations, and what you have read so far.
2. Tell what you think will happen next—or what you will learn. Thinking about what you already know about the subject may help.
3. Try to figure out things the author does not say directly.

Listen as your teacher begins "The Rule." When your teacher stops, complete the activity with a partner to show that you understand how to predict what you think might happen in the story.

Think about the story and respond to the question below.

What do you think might happen in the story?

_____

_____

As you continue listening to the story, think about whether your prediction was right. You might want to change your prediction or write a new one below.

_____

_____

_____

Name _____

Strategy 2: Phonics/Decoding

Use this strategy during reading when you come across a word you don't know.

Here's how to use the Phonics/Decoding strategy:

1. Look carefully at the word.
2. Look for word parts that you know and think about the sounds for the letters.
3. Blend the sounds to read the word.
4. Ask yourself if this is a word you know and whether the word makes sense in the sentence.
5. If not, ask yourself if there is anything else you could try—should you look in the dictionary?

Listen as your teacher continues to read the story. When your teacher stops, use the Phonics/Decoding strategy.

Now write down the steps you used to decode the word *trout*.

_____

_____

_____

_____

_____

_____

Remember to use this strategy whenever you are reading and come across a word that you don't know.

Name _____

Strategy 3: Monitor/Clarify

Use this strategy during reading whenever you're confused about what you are reading.

Here's how to use the Monitor/Clarify strategy:
- Ask yourself if what you're reading makes sense—or if you are learning what you need to learn.
- If you don't understand something, reread, look at the illustrations, or read ahead to see if that helps.

Listen as your teacher continues to read the story. When your teacher stops, complete the activity with a partner to show that you understand how to figure out why the boy in the story might think the mushrooms look like a forest.

Think about the story and respond below.

1. Have you ever eaten mushrooms? What do they look like?

_____

_____

2. Can you tell from listening to the story why the boy may have thought the mushrooms looked like a forest? Why or why not?

_____

_____

3. How can you find out why he may have thought that?

_____

_____

Name _____

Strategy 4: Question

Use this strategy during and after reading to ask questions about important ideas in the story.

Here's how to use the Question strategy:
- Ask yourself questions about important ideas in the story.
- Ask yourself if you can answer these questions.
- If you can't answer the questions, reread and look for answers in the text. Thinking about what you already know and what you've read in the story may help you.

Listen as your teacher continues to read the story. Then complete the activity with a partner to show that you understand how to ask yourself questions about important ideas in the story.

Think about the story and respond below.

Write a question you might ask yourself at this point in the story.

_____

_____

_____

_____

_____

If you can't answer your question now, think about it while you listen to the rest of the story.

Name _____

Strategy 5: Evaluate

Use this strategy during and after reading to help you form an opinion about what you read.

Here's how to use the Evaluate strategy:

- Think about how the author makes the story come alive and makes you want to read it.
- Think about what was entertaining, informative, or useful about the selection.
- Think about how you reacted to the story—how well you understood the selection and whether you enjoyed reading it.

Listen as your teacher continues to read the story. When your teacher stops, complete the activity with a partner to show that you are thinking of how you feel about what you are reading and why you feel that way.

Think about the story and respond below.

1. Tell whether or not you think this story is entertaining and why.

_____

_____

2. This is a humorous, realistic fiction story. Did the author make the characters interesting and believable?

_____

_____

3. How did you react to this story?

_____

Name _____

Strategy 6: Summarize

Use this strategy after reading to summarize what you read.

Here's how to use the Summarize strategy:

- Think about the characters.
- Think about where the story takes place.
- Think about the problem in the story and how the characters solve it.
- Think about what happens in the beginning, middle, and end of the story.

Think about the story you just listened to. Complete the activity with a partner to show that you understand how to identify important story parts that will help you summarize the story.

Think about the story and respond to the questions below:

1. Who is the main character?

_____

_____

2. Where does the story take place?

_____

_____

3. What is the problem and how is it resolved?

_____

_____

Now use this information to summarize the story for a partner.

8

Name _____

Off to Adventure!

Cut out a picture of something you think is an adventure from a magazine or a newspaper. Paste it on this page. Then answer the questions below. Answers will vary.

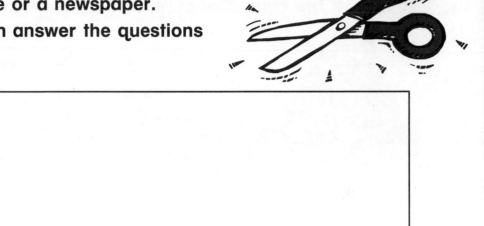

1. What do you think makes this an adventure?

   (3 points) _____

   _____

2. How would you describe this adventure to someone?

   (3) _____

   _____

3. Would you like to be part of this adventure? Explain your answer.

   (4) _____

   _____

Name _____

Off to Adventure!

As you read each selection in *Off to Adventure!*, fill in the boxes of the chart that apply to the selection. Sample answers shown.

(5 points per selection)

	How does the adventure begin?	How do the characters change by the end of the adventure?
Cliff Hanger	A dog gets trapped on a cliff. **(2 points)**	The boy finds the courage to make a dangerous rescue. **(3)**
The Ballad of Mulan	Mulan joins the army in her father's place. **(2)**	Mulan shows courage and becomes a general. **(3)**
The Lost and Found	Three students disappear into the school's Lost and Found. **(2)**	Wendell, Floyd, and Mona have become friends. **(3)**

Assessment Tip: Total **15** Points

Name _____

Adventure Advertisement

Help rewrite this ad to make it more exciting. Replace the words in parentheses with words from the box. Fill in the blanks with the correct words.

Vocabulary

1. belay
2. descent
3. harness
4. ledge
5. rappel
6. trekked

Try rock climbing in the Teton Mountains! After you have <u>trekked **(1 point)**</u> (made a slow and difficult journey on foot) to the base of a cliff, put on your <u>harness **(1)**</u> (set of straps that can attach to a safety rope). Make sure to climb on <u>belay **(1)**</u> (tied to a person or a rock with a rope for safety) so you don't fall. If you get tired on the way up, find a <u>ledge **(1)**</u> (shelf of rock) and take a rest. Then get ready for your <u>descent **(1)**</u> (a trip down into or from something, such as a mountain). If you really want a thrill, you can <u>rappel **(1)**</u> (climb down from a steep height) back to the ground.

Describe how to rappel. (Hint: If you need help, look at pages 16–17 in your textbook.) (2 points)

Attach a rope to a rock and to your harness and lower

yourself to the ground.

Name _____

Cause-and-Effect Chart

Cause (Why does it happen?)	Effect (What happens?)
Climbers leave Grits on the mountain. **(2 points)**	Axel and Dag set out to rescue Grits.
He thinks Grits might fall from Monkey Ledge. **(2)**	Axel decides to climb up and get Grits in spite of the storm.
Axel climbs carefully, using all the proper equipment.	He reaches Monkey Ledge safely. **(2)**
Electricity from the storm fills the air. **(2)**	The hair on Axel's head and arms stands up.
Partway down the cliff, Axel runs out of rope.	He free climbs the rest of the way down. **(2)**

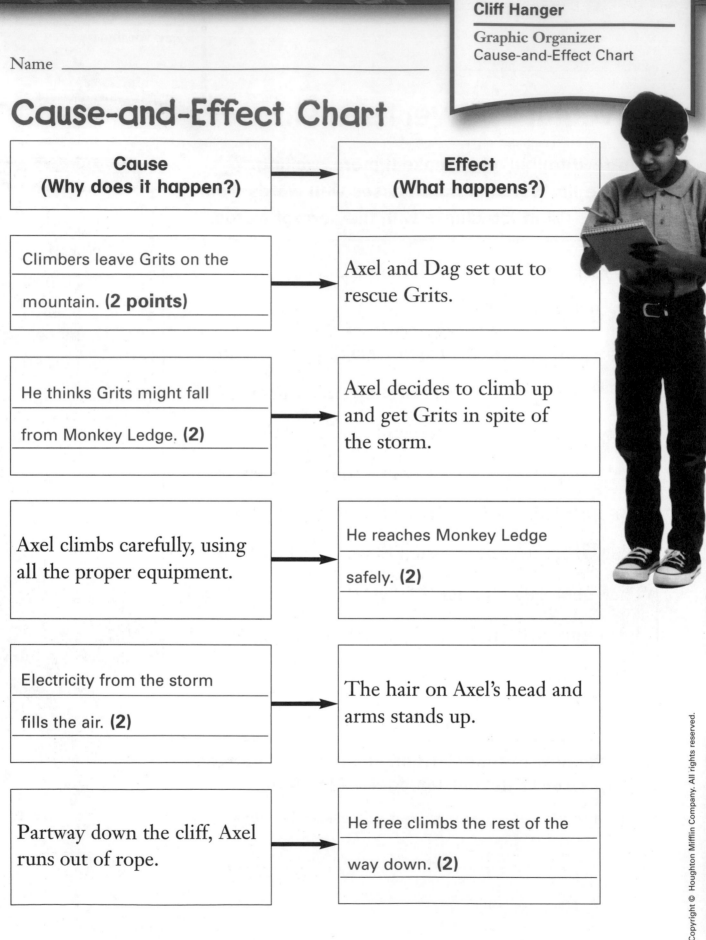

Assessment Tip: Total **10** Points

Name _____

Finish the Story

Complete each of the sentences with details from
Cliff Hanger.

1. Axel's dog, Grits, <u>gets stranded on Cathedral Wall. **(1 point)**</u>
_____

2. Dag tells Axel that the storm is still far enough away
   <u>to rescue Grits **(1)**</u>
   _____

3. Dag changes his mind and tells Axel not to climb, but
   <u>Axel starts climbing anyway. **(1)**</u>

4. Axel reaches Grits safely and <u>waits till the storm has passed.</u>
   (1)

5. He lowers Grits down on a rope, but <u>doesn't have enough</u>
   <u>rope left to rappel down. **(1)**</u>

6. Axel rappels halfway down and <u>free climbs the rest of</u>
   <u>the way. **(1)**</u>

Theme 1: **Off to Adventure!**   13
Assessment Tip: Total **6** Points

Name _____

Causes and Effects

**Read the story. Think about what happens and why.
Then complete the chart on the next page.**

The Tornado

A rooster crowed, waking Lucy Sunders from a deep sleep.
She usually popped out of bed like buttons pop off a shirt, but
today she was tired. She had stayed up late last night reading.

Lucy looked out her window. The sky was a funny yellow-
gray, and there were no sounds. Then, across the fields, Lucy
saw a whirling dust cloud. It grew bigger and bigger. A
tornado was coming!

Lucy raced down the stairs, shouting, "Mama, Mama —
a tornado!"

Mrs. Sunders checked the sky. Then she grabbed the baby
from his swing. "Run! Run to the root cellar!" she shouted.

Lucy and her mother ran through the yard, and Lucy
pulled open the cellar door. She hurried down the steps. Her
mother locked the door and followed her into the darkness.

Quickly Mrs. Sunders lit the old lamp, and the light
glowed warmly. Lucy sighed. They were safe now.
Everything would be all right.

Name _____

Causes and Effects continued

In each box, write a cause or an effect from the story.

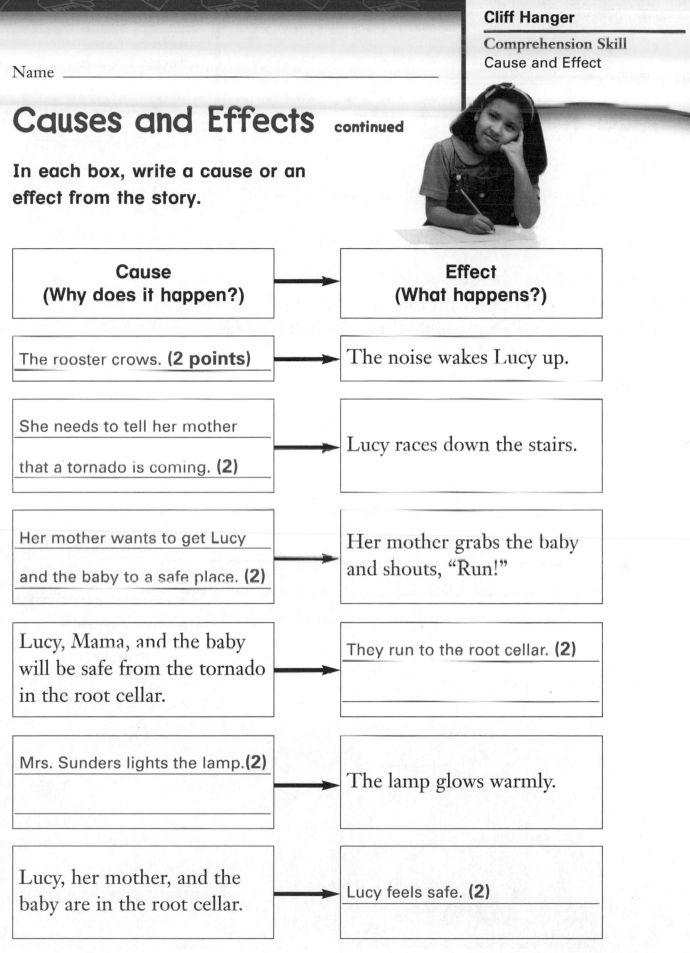

Cause **(Why does it happen?)**	**Effect** **(What happens?)**
The rooster crows. **(2 points)**	The noise wakes Lucy up.
She needs to tell her mother that a tornado is coming. **(2)**	Lucy races down the stairs.
Her mother wants to get Lucy and the baby to a safe place. **(2)**	Her mother grabs the baby and shouts, "Run!"
Lucy, Mama, and the baby will be safe from the tornado in the root cellar.	They run to the root cellar. **(2)**
Mrs. Sunders lights the lamp.**(2)**	The lamp glows warmly.
Lucy, her mother, and the baby are in the root cellar.	Lucy feels safe. **(2)**

Name _____

Add the Ending

► For words that end with a vowel and a single
consonant, double the consonant before adding
-ed or -ing.

grip + p + ed = gripped   swim + m + ing = swimming

**Read the clues for the puzzle. For each one, choose
a word from the box with the same meaning as the
word in dark type. Complete the puzzle by adding
-ed or -ing to the word from the box.**

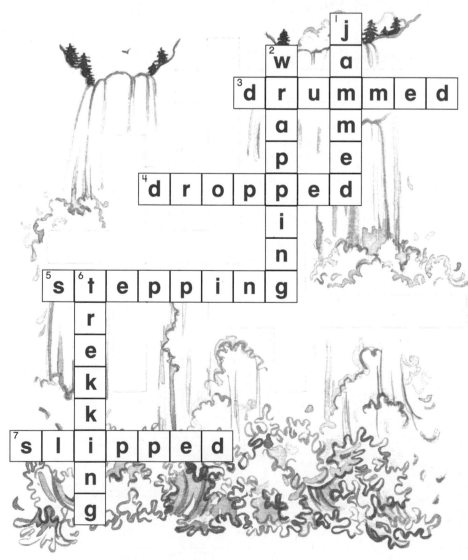

Across

3. The thunder **boomed**
loudly while lightning
exploded.
4. The temperature **fell**
suddenly.
5. The dog was **moving**
forward carefully.
7. His hand **slid** from
the ledge.

Down

1. Axel **stuck** his fist in a
crack.
2. Dag was **winding** the
rope around his waist.
6. They had never liked
hiking over the trails.

Name _____

Short Vowels

► A short vowel sound is usually spelled with one
vowel followed by a consonant sound.

    The /ă/ sound is usually spelled **a,** as in l**a**st.

    The /ě/ sound is usually spelled **e,** as in sm**e**ll.

    The /ĭ/ sound is usually spelled **i,** as in m**i**x.

► Sometimes the /ě/ sound is spelled in a different way.
In the starred words *head* and *friend*, the /ě/ sound is
spelled *ea* and *ie*.

Write each Spelling Word under its vowel sound.
Order of answers for each category may vary.

Spelling Words
1. mix*
2. milk
3. smell
4. last
5. head
6. friend*
7. class
8. left
9. thick
10. send
11. thin
12. stick

/ă/ Sound

last **(1 point)**

class **(1)**

/ě/ Sound

smell **(1)**

head **(1)**

friend **(1)**

left **(1)**

send **(1)**

/ĭ/ Sound

mix **(1)**

milk **(1)**

thick **(1)**

thin **(1)**

stick **(1)**

Theme 1: **Off to Adventure!**   17

Assessment Tip: Total **12** Points

Name _____

Spelling Spree

Silly Rhymes Write a Spelling Word to complete each silly sentence. Each answer rhymes with the underlined word.

1. Will chewing gum _____ to a <u>brick</u>?
2. Don't pile <u>bread</u> on your _____!
3. Never drink _____ while wearing <u>silk</u>.
4. You have to be _____ to squeeze under a <u>bin</u>.
5. <u>Fix</u> the ladder and _____ the batter.
6. How can you <u>tell</u> if bees can _____?

1. <u>stick</u> **(1 point)**
2. <u>head</u> **(1)**
3. <u>milk</u> **(1)**
4. <u>thin</u> **(1)**
5. <u>mix</u> **(1)**
6. <u>smell</u> **(1)**

Letter Math Write a Spelling Word by adding and taking away letters from the words below.

Example: d + fish - f = *dish*

7. spend - p   = <u>send</u> **(1)**
8. c + glass - g = <u>class</u> **(1)**
9. leg - g + ft   = <u>left</u> **(1)**
10. fri + mend - m = <u>friend</u> **(1)**
11. blast - b   = <u>last</u> **(1)**
12. th + sick - s = <u>thick</u> **(1)**

Assessment Tip: Total **12** Points

Proofreading and Writing

Proofreading Circle the five misspelled Spelling Words in the following notice. Then write each word correctly.

1. mix*
2. milk
3. smell
4. last
5. head
6. friend*
7. class
8. left
9. thick
10. send
11. thin
12. stick

Attention All Visitors

People come from many countries to hike in our wilderness areas and (smel) the clean mountain air. Please show your respect for this natural world. Be careful on the trails, and always hike with a (freind). A hiking (stik) is a good idea too. Bring a (thik) sweater, and wear a hat to protect your (hed) from rain or sun. Enjoy your visit!

1. smell **(2 points)**

2. friend **(2)**

3. stick **(2)**

4. thick **(2)**

5. head **(2)**

Write a Journal Entry Think about a special time you had outdoors. Where were you? Was it a field trip? A family outing? Or maybe a block party?

On a separate sheet of paper, describe where you were and what was special about the experience. Use Spelling Words from the list. Responses will vary. **(5)**

Theme 1: **Off to Adventure!**   19
Assessment Tip: Total **15** Points

Name _____

Name _____

Find the Right Order

The words on List 1 appear in any old order. Put the words in alphabetical order and write them on List 2.

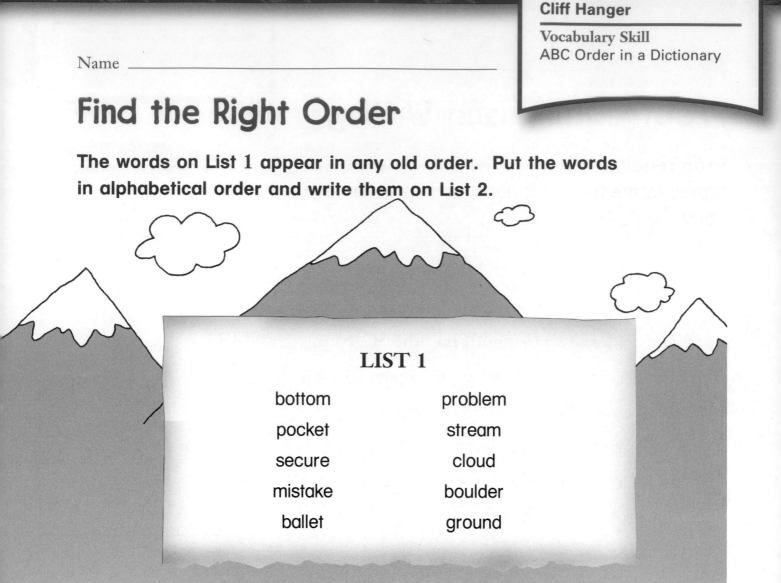

LIST 1

bottom	problem
pocket	stream
secure	cloud
mistake	boulder
ballet	ground

LIST 2

1. ballet **(1 point)**
2. bottom **(1)**
3. boulder **(1)**
4. cloud **(1)**
5. ground **(1)**

6. mistake **(1)**
7. pocket **(1)**
8. problem **(1)**
9. secure **(1)**
10. stream **(1)**

Assessment Tip: Total **10** Points

Name _____

Finding Sentences

Read each group of words. Write *sentence* if the words form a complete sentence. Write *fragment* if the words do not form a complete sentence. Then rewrite each fragment as a complete sentence. Add a word from the box at the bottom of the page.

1. A big storm was coming fast. <u>sentence</u> **(2 points)**

_____

2. The frightened dog. <u>fragment</u> _____

   The frightened dog howled. **(2)**

3. Climbed slowly up the ledge. <u>fragment</u> _____

   Axel climbed slowly up the ledge. **(2)**

4. Axel saved Grits. <u>sentence</u> **(2)**

_____

5. A bolt of lightning. <u>fragment</u> _____

   A bolt of lightning flashed. **(2)**

6. Heated on the stove. <u>fragment</u> _____

   Soup heated on the stove. **(2)**

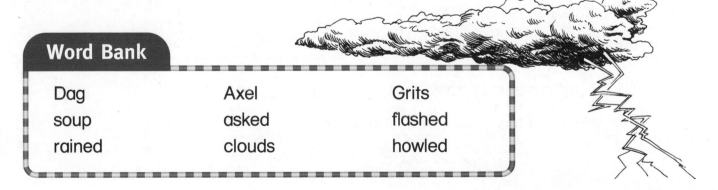

Word Bank

Dag	Axel	Grits
soup	asked	flashed
rained	clouds	howled

Theme 1: **Off to Adventure!**   21
Assessment Tip: Total **12** Points

Name _____

Changing Fragments into Sentences

Correct each fragment below to make a complete sentence.
Answers will vary. Suggested sentences given.

1. Axel and his father

   Axel and his father like rock climbing. **(2 points)**

2. was worried about his dog

   Axel was worried about his dog. **(2)**

3. in the sky

   Clouds gathered in the sky. **(2)**

4. carried gear for rock climbing

   Dag and Axel carried gear for rock climbing. **(2)**

5. down the trail

   Hikers hurried down the trail. **(2)**

6. a dangerous ledge

   Axel climbed a dangerous ledge. **(2)**

7. lots of rain

   Lots of rain fell on the mountain. **(2)**

8. had a big adventure that day

   The boy had a big adventure that day. **(2)**

Assessment Tip: Total **16** Points

Name _____

Finding Sentences

**Effective writers use complete sentences. Correct each
sentence fragment. Write your revised sentence on the line.
If the sentence is already complete, write the word** *correct*.

Answers will vary for items 5 and 7. Suggested sentences given.

A Day in the Life of Grits

1. I went for a walk. On a steep trail.

   I went for a walk on a steep trail. **(2 points)**

2. In the warm sunshine, I wagged my tail.

   correct **(2)**

3. Then I heard thunder.

   correct **(2)**

4. The sky. Grew dark.

   The sky grew dark. **(2)**

5. Whimpered, howled, and barked.

   I whimpered, howled, and barked. **(2)**

6. Then Axel climbed. Up the rock.

   Then Axel climbed up the rock. **(2)**

I would thank him
if I could talk!

7. Hugged me.

   He hugged me. **(2)**

8. I felt safe.

   correct **(2)**

Name _____

Reasons and Facts

Use this page to plan your explanation. Then number your reasons or facts in the order you will use them.

Topic: **(2 points)** _____

_____

_____

Topic Sentence: **(2)** _____

_____

_____

Reason/Fact: **(2)** _____   Reason/Fact: **(2)** _____

_____   _____

_____   _____

Reason/Fact: **(2)** _____   Reason/Fact: **(2)** _____

_____   _____

_____   _____

Assessment Tip: Total **12** Points

Name _____

Improving Your Writing

► Sometimes questions can be changed into statements by moving the words around.
Are the children's parents good climbers?
The children's parents are good climbers.

► Sometimes words must be added, removed, or changed to make a question into a statement.
Did most readers like the story?
Most readers liked the story.

► Changing the question on a test into a statement can help you write a good topic sentence and focus your ideas.
Why is climbing exciting?
There are several reason why climbing is exciting.

Change each question into a statement.
Answers will vary. Possible answers are given.

1. What are some of the family's favorite activities?

   The family has several favorite activities. **(2 points)**

2. Did everyone in the class like the action story?

   Everyone in the class liked the action story. **(2)**

3. Who are the main characters in this story?

   There are several main characters in this story. [Names of

   characters] are the main characters in this story. **(2)**

4. Why is swimming under a waterfall fun?

   Swimming under a waterfall is fun for a number of reasons.**(2)**

5. What types of movies does their family like to see?

   Their family likes to see several types of movies. **(2)**

Name _____

Revising Your Personal Narrative

Reread your paper. Put a checkmark in the box for each sentence that describes your paper. Use this page to help you revise.

Rings the Bell

☐ The beginning catches the reader's interest.

☐ Many details and exact words bring the story to life.

☐ Everything is told in order and keeps to the topic.

☐ My writing sounds like me. You can tell how I feel.

☐ Sentences are different lengths. There are few mistakes.

Getting Stronger

☐ The beginning could be more interesting.

☐ More details and exact words are needed.

☐ A few events are out of order, and a few are unrelated.

☐ My voice could be stronger. It doesn't always sound like me.

☐ Many sentences are short. There are some mistakes.

Try Harder

☐ The beginning is missing or weak.

☐ There are no details or exact words.

☐ The story is not focused. The order is unclear.

☐ I can't hear my voice at all.

☐ All my sentences are short. Mistakes make it hard to read.

Name _____

Combining Sentences

Combine each pair of sentences into one. Include all the important parts of both sentences. Avoid repeating words.

1. The water was cold. The water was full of sharks.

   The water was cold and full of sharks. **(2 points)**

   _____

2. Nina dove in the water. Brenda dove in the water.

   Nina and Brenda dove in the water. **(2)**

   _____

3. Paul screamed. Winston screamed.

   Paul and Winston screamed. **(2)**

4. Nina laughed. Nina shouted, "Come on in, fellas!"

   Nina laughed and shouted, "Come on in, fellas!" **(2)**

   _____

5. Paul said, "No way!" Winston said, "No way!"

   Paul and Winston said, "No way!" **(2)**

   _____

6. Brenda yelled, "These sharks are only toys!" Nina yelled, "These sharks are only toys!"

   Brenda and Nina yelled, "These sharks are only toys!" **(2)**

   _____

Assessment Tip: Total **12** Points

Name _____

Spelling Words

Look for spelling patterns you have learned to help you remember the Spelling Words on this page. Think about the parts that you find hard to spell.

Write the missing letters and apostrophe in the Spelling Words below. Order of answers for 6 and 7 may vary.

1. hav e_____ **(1 point)**

2. hav e_____ n_____ '_____ t_____ **(1)**

3. f o_____ u_____ nd **(1)**

4. ar o_____ u_____ nd **(1)**

5. o_____ ne **(1)**

6. th a_____ n **(1)**

7. th e_____ n **(1)**

8. th e_____ m **(1)**

9. befo r_____ e_____ **(1)**

10. bec a_____ u_____ s_____ e **(1)**

11. o_____ ther **(1)**

12. m_____ o_____ ther **(1)**

Study List On another sheet of paper, write each Spelling Word. Check the list to be sure you spell each word correctly. Order of words may vary. **(2)**

Spelling Words

1. have
2. haven't
3. found
4. around
5. one
6. than
7. then
8. them
9. before
10. because
11. other
12. mother

28   Theme 1: **Off to Adventure!**
Assessment Tip: Total **14** Points

Name _____

Spelling Spree

Sentence Fillers Write the Spelling Word from the list on this page that best completes each sentence.

1–2. "Scott, _____ you seen my coat?"

"No, I _____."

3. We drove _____ the block three times.

4. Our neighbors asked us to lend _____ our lawnmower.

5. For a while it was noisy, but _____ it got quiet.

6. We met at the theater _____ the movie started.

7. I don't want this one, I want the _____ one.

8. Tania _____ a five-dollar bill lying on the ground.

Spelling Words

1. have
2. haven't
3. found
4. around
5. one
6. than
7. then
8. them
9. before
10. because
11. other
12. mother

1. have **(1 point)**

2. haven't **(1)**

3. around **(1)**

4. them **(1)**

5. then **(1)**

6. before **(1)**

7. other **(1)**

8. found **(1)**

Word Clues Write the Spelling Word that fits each clue best.

9. You can use this word when you give a reason.

10. This word isn't a father, but a _____.

11. This word is the first thing you say when you count.

12. You can use this word when you compare two things.

9. because **(1)**

10. mother **(1)**

11. one **(1)**

12. than **(1)**

Theme 1: **Off to Adventure!** 29

Assessment Tip: Total **12** Points

Name _____

Proofreading and Writing

Proofreading Circle the four misspelled Spelling Words in this postcard. Then write each word correctly on the lines below.

Spelling Words

1. have
2. haven't
3. found
4. around
5. one
6. than
7. then
8. them
9. before
10. because
11. other
12. mother

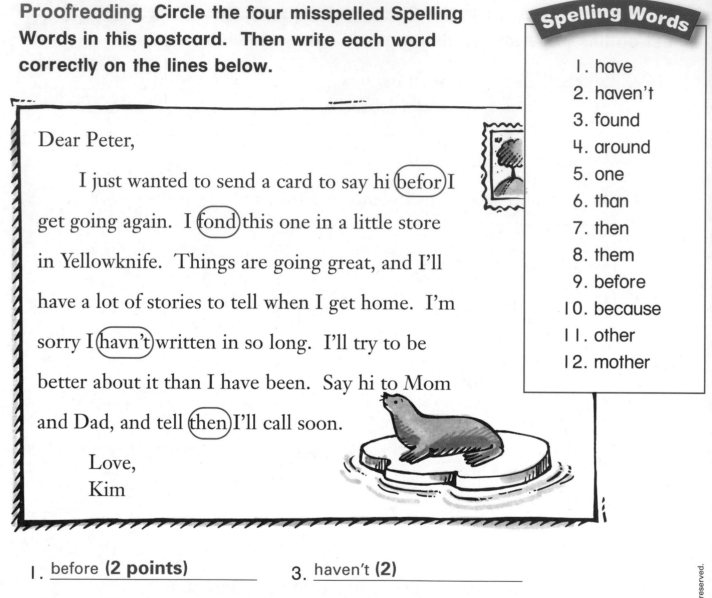

Dear Peter,

I just wanted to send a card to say hi (befor) I get going again. I (fond) this one in a little store in Yellowknife. Things are going great, and I'll have a lot of stories to tell when I get home. I'm sorry I (havn't) written in so long. I'll try to be better about it than I have been. Say hi to Mom and Dad, and tell (then) I'll call soon.

Love,
Kim

1. before **(2 points)**

2. found **(2)**

3. haven't **(2)**

4. them **(2)**

Adventure Dialogue Get together with another student and write a dialogue about an adventure. Both people in the dialogue can be off adventuring, or you can have one of them stay at home. Use Spelling Words from the list.

Responses will vary. **(2)**

Assessment Tip: Total **10** Points

Name _____

Crossword Challenge!

Write the word that matches each clue in the puzzle.
Use the words in the box and your glossary for help.

Vocabulary

armor	comrades	endured	farewell
triumphant	troops	victorious	

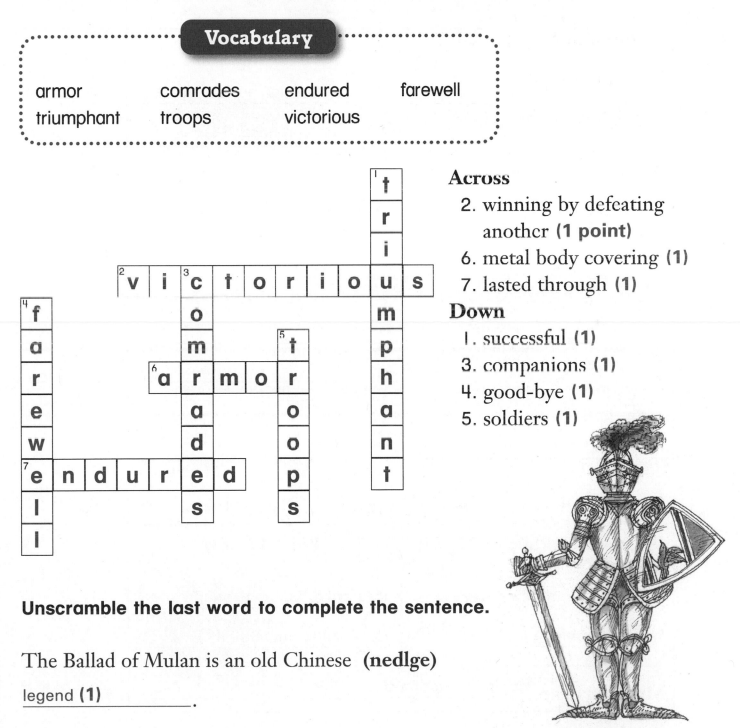

Across

2. winning by defeating another **(1 point)**
6. metal body covering **(1)**
7. lasted through **(1)**

Down

1. successful **(1)**
3. companions **(1)**
4. good-bye **(1)**
5. soldiers **(1)**

Puzzle answers:

1. triumphant (down)
2. victorious (across)
3. comrades (down)
4. farewell (down)
5. troops (down)
6. armor (across)
7. endured (across)

Unscramble the last word to complete the sentence.

The Ballad of Mulan is an old Chinese **(nedlge)**

legend **(1)**
_____.

Name _____

Inference Chart

Responses will vary.

---

1. At the beginning of the story, how does Mulan feel?

Story Clues (pages 56–57)	**What I Know**
She stops weaving. She sighs sorrowfully. **(1)**	People who sigh sorrowfully are often sad and upset. **(1)**

My Inference _Mulan feels sad and upset._ **(2)**

---

2. Why does Mulan decide to help her father?

Story Clues (pages 58–61)	**What I Know**
Her father is drafted into the army. He is old and frail. **(2)**	War is dangerous, especially to the old, frail people. **(1)**

My Inference _She fears that her father will get hurt or killed._ **(2)**

---

3. Years later, how does the Emperor feel about Mulan?

Story Clues (pages 72–73)	**What I Know**
She is praised for her bravery and leadership in battle. **(3)**	It's hard to be brave and be a good leader in battle. **(1)**

My Inference _Mulan is a hero._ **(2)**

---

32   Theme 1: **Off to Adventure!**
Assessment Tip: Total **15** Points

Name _____

Answers About Mulan

Answer these questions about *The Ballad of Mulan*.

1. Why does the Emperor need troops?

   An enemy army is attacking China. **(2 points)**

   _____

2. Why does Mulan go to war in her father's place?

   She has no older brother; her father is old and frail. **(2)**

   _____

3. After the war, why does the Emperor want to honor Mulan?

   Her skill, bravery, and leadership have helped to win battles. **(2)**

   _____

4. How does Mulan's family feel about having her come home?

   They are excited and proud; the parents come out to welcome her; her sister

   beautifies herself; her brother helps to prepare a feast. **(2)**

5. When Mulan returns home, what does she choose to do?

   She changes from her armor into a favorite dress. **(2)**

   _____

6. What is the meaning of Mulan's statement about the rabbits?

   Accept reasonable responses. Example: In times of danger, how you act is

   more important than whether you are a man or woman. **(2)**

7. Why do the Chinese still honor Mulan?

   Accept reasonable responses. Example: She showed love and respect

   for her family and country without asking for a reward. **(3)**

Theme 1: **Off to Adventure!** 33
Assessment Tip: Total **15** Points

Name _____

Make a Good Guess

Read the story below. Then answer the questions on the following page.

The Ice Girl

Trolls were raiding the valley. They swooped down from icy mountain caves, looking for workers and burning houses and barns. Those unlucky enough to be caught never saw daylight again. The people in the valley called a meeting to deal with the problem.

Greta sat and knitted. Ever since Father had fallen, Brother was doing all the family chores. Even at this late hour, he had gone to town while Father slept. Greta helped as best she could. In her spare time, she knitted and knitted. Perhaps her work would help to keep them from selling a cow.

Suddenly, Greta heard a noise outside. Trolls! She slipped out a side door and stood waiting. Sure enough, four ugly trolls peered around the barn. Greta stood still. Slowly the trolls crept closer and closer, but Greta never moved. Finally she felt the steam from their mouths. Then she gathered all her strength and yelled, "Boo!" as loud as she could. The trolls jumped. Then they ran off, as fast as their feet could move. From that day on, no troll ever came back to the valley again.

And to this day, people remember her deed. They have even put up a sign. It reads, "Here is where Greta, the Ice Girl, once lived. She drove the trolls away by saying 'Boo!'"

Name _____

Make a Good Guess continued

Use clues from the story and what you know to answer each question below.

1. What did the people want to do about the trolls?

   They wanted to find a way to stop the trolls or get rid of them. **(2 points)**

   _____

2. What happened to people who were caught by the trolls?

   They had to work for the trolls in their caves. **(2)**

   _____

3. Why did Brother have to do all the family chores?

   Father was hurt badly when he fell. **(2)**

   _____

4. Why did Greta spend so much time knitting?

   She hoped to make money selling hand-knit things, so the family wouldn't

   have to sell a cow. **(2)**

5. At the end, why were no trolls ever seen in the valley again?

   Greta's actions scared them away. **(2)**

Assessment Tip: Total **10** Points

Name _____

Syllabication

If you come across a word you can't pronounce, try dividing the word into **syllables**, or parts of a word that are said out loud as single sounds. Each word below has two syllables. Each can be divided in a different way.

Divide the compound word into two words:

sunrise = sun • rise

Divide the word between two consonants:

village = vil • lage

Write the words below with spaces between the two syllables. Divide them either between the words in a compound word or between two consonants.

1. mirror   mir   ror **(1 point)** _____

     between two consonants **(1)** _____

2. nightfall   night   fall **(1)** _____

     between two words **(1)** _____

3. poster   post   er **(1)** _____

     between two consonants **(1)** _____

4. mountain   moun   tain **(1)** _____

     between two consonants **(1)** _____

5. downtown   down   town **(1)** _____

     between two words **(1)** _____

Assessment Tip: Total **10** Points

Name _____

More Short Vowels

A short vowel sound is usually spelled with one vowel followed by a consonant sound.

   The /ŏ/ sound is usually spelled o, as in lot.
   The /ŭ/ sound is usually spelled u, as in rub.

▶ Sometimes the /ŭ/ sound is spelled in a different way. In the starred words *does* and *won*, the /ŭ/ sound is spelled *oe* and *o*.

Write each Spelling Word under its vowel sound.
Order of answers for each category may vary.

/ŏ/ Sound
pond **(1 point)**

drop **(1)**

lot **(1)**

sock **(1)**

crop **(1)**

/ŭ/ Sound
luck **(1)**

rub **(1)**

does **(1)**

drum **(1)**

hunt **(1)**

shut **(1)**

won **(1)**

Name _____

Spelling Spree

Finding Words Write the Spelling Word hidden in each of these words.

1. shutter   <u>shut **(1 point)**</u>

2. wonderful   <u>won **(1)**</u>

3. plot   <u>lot **(1)**</u>

4. rubber   <u>rub **(1)**</u>

5. doesn't   <u>does **(1)**</u>

6. eardrum   <u>drum **(1)**</u>

Questions Write a Spelling Word to answer each question.

1. pond
2. luck
3. drop
4. lot
5. rub
6. does*
7. drum
8. sock
9. hunt
10. crop
11. shut
12. won*

7. What do you wear inside a shoe?

8. What does a farmer grow?

9. What can help you win a game?

10. What body of water is smaller than a lake?

11. What do lions do to get their dinner?

12. What do you call a tiny bead of water?

7. <u>sock **(1 point)**</u>   10. <u>pond **(1)**</u>

8. <u>crop **(1)**</u>   11. <u>hunt **(1)**</u>

9. <u>luck **(1)**</u>   12. <u>drop **(1)**</u>

Assessment Tip: Total **12** Points

Name _____

Proofreading and Writing

Proofreading Circle the five misspelled Spelling Words below. Then write each word correctly.

The Emperor Praises Mulan

The Emperor welcomed General Mulan to the High Palace today. First, a soldier played a huge (drume). Then the Emperor gave a speech. He told how Mulan was willing to (droppe) everything to join the army. He said the famous general did not win battles by (luk) but by skill and bravery. Now, thanks to Mulan, the war is (wone). No longer (dose) an invading army threaten China. The gates of the Great Wall are safely shut.

Spelling Words

1. pond
2. luck
3. drop
4. lot
5. rub
6. does*
7. drum
8. sock
9. hunt
10. crop
11. shut
12. won*

1. drum **(1 point)**

2. drop **(1)**

3. luck **(1)**

4. won **(1)**

5. does **(1)**

Write a Story Long ago, in a land far away, a brave young girl named Mulan began a dangerous adventure. How would you begin an adventure story? What setting would you use? It could be a dark jungle or a distant planet, or it might be your own neighborhood.

On a separate sheet of paper, write the opening paragraph of an adventure story. Use Spelling Words from the list. Responses will vary. **(5)**

Assessment Tip: Total **10** Points

Name _____

Multiple Meaning Words

long *adjective* **1.** Having great length: *a long river.*
2. Lasting for a large amount of time: *a long movie.*
3. Lasting a certain length: *The show was an hour long.*
♦ *adverb* Far away in the past: *The dinosaurs lived long ago.*
♦ *verb* To wish or want very much: *The children longed for an ice cream cone.*

For each of the following sentences, choose the correct definition of the underlined word. Write the definition on the line.

1. <u>Long</u> ago, a girl named Mulan went into battle.

   far away in the past **(1 point)**

2. A <u>long</u> line of soldiers crossed the mountain.

   having great length **(1)**

3. The town <u>longed</u> for peace to return.

   to wish or want very much **(1)**

4. It was a <u>long</u> way to the Yellow River.

   having great length **(1)**

5. Mulan <u>longed</u> to hear her mother's voice.

   to wish or want very much **(1)**

6. The war was ten years <u>long</u>.

   lasting a certain length **(1)**

Assessment Tip: Total **6** Points

Classifying Sentences

Read and classify each sentence. Write *statement*, *question*, *command*, or *exclamation* on the line provided.

1. Why did Mulan fight in the army? <u>question **(1 point)**</u>

2. What an amazing girl she is! <u>exclamation **(1)**</u>

3. Tell me what her journey was like. <u>command **(1)**</u>

4. She was surrounded by many dangers. <u>statement **(1)**</u>

5. Mulan's family and friends were very proud of her.

   <u>statement **(1)**</u>

6. There she goes now! <u>exclamation **(1)**</u>

7. Watch the victory parade. <u>command **(1)**</u>

8. Can you see Mulan at the front of the troops?

   <u>question **(1)**</u>

9. The musicians sing a song about Mulan's

   adventures. <u>statement **(1)**</u>

10. How beautiful the music sounds!

    <u>exclamation **(1)**</u>

Name _____

Arranging Sentences

Arrange these sentences to create an interview with Mulan. Four of the sentences are questions and four are the answers to these questions. On the lines below, write each question followed by its answer. Add the correct end marks.

I dressed in armor	I was terrified at first
Were you afraid	Why did you join the army
My father was too ill to fight	Look at my face and see how
Are you glad to be home	happy I am
	What did you wear

The order of the questions and answers may vary.

1. **Q:** Why did you join the army? **(1 point)**

   A: My father was too ill to fight. **(1)**

2. **Q:** Were you afraid? **(1)**

   A: I was terrified at first! **(1)**

3. **Q:** What did you wear? **(1)**

   A: I dressed in armor. **(1)**

4. **Q:** Are you glad to be home? **(1)**

   A: Look at my face and see how happy I am. **(1)**

Assessment Tip: Total **8** Points

Name _____

Capitalizing and Punctuating Sentences

Capital letters and punctuation help us to understand writing. Three students decided to act out a scene from *The Ballad of Mulan*. Here is the script they wrote for the scene. Check the capitalization and punctuation of each sentence. Then rewrite the script, using the correct capitalization and punctuation.

Soldier 1: Mulan, is that really you

1. Mulan, is that really you? **(2 points)**

Soldier 2: how is this possible

2. How is this possible? **(2)**

Soldier 1: are you really a girl

3. Are you really a girl? **(2)**

Mulan: yes, I am you have not seen the real me

4. Yes, I am. You have not seen the real me. **(2)**

Soldier 1: you are brave and amazing

5. You are brave and amazing! **(2)**

Soldier 2: what a remarkable girl you are

6. What a remarkable girl you are! **(2)**

Mulan: I had to save my father would you have let me fight if I had dressed as a woman

7. I had to save my father. Would you have let me fight if I had

   dressed as a woman? **(2)**

Name _____

Response Journal

Writing a Response Journal Entry Write about a story you
are reading now. Answer the questions. Use your own ideas.

Title of Story Responses will vary. **(1 point)**

How do I feel about what happens in the story?

Responses will vary. **(1)**

_____

How do I feel about the main character?

Responses will vary. **(1)**

_____

What do I think will happen next in the story?

Responses will vary. **(1)**

_____

What puzzles me about the story?

Responses will vary. **(1)**

_____

Which character in the story is most like me? Why?

Responses will vary. **(1)**

_____

Assessment Tip: Total **6** Points

Name _____

Capitalizing Days and Months

► Begin an entry in your journal with the day or date.
► Begin the name of the day of the week with a capital letter.

     Monday   **T**uesday   **W**ednesday   **T**hursday
     Friday   **S**aturday   **S**unday

► Begin the months of the year with capital letters.

     April 12
     November 24

Write each day or date correctly.

1. wednesday — Wednesday **(1 point)**

2. friday, november 18 — Friday, November 18 **(2)**

3. saturday — Saturday **(1)**

4. monday, january 7 — Monday, January 7 **(2)**

5. thursday — Thursday **(1)**

6. tuesday, may 8 — Tuesday, May 8 **(2)**

7. sunday — Sunday **(1)**

Name _____

What a Day!

Joey has just moved to a new town. Help him finish a letter to his friend. Fill in the blanks with the correct words from the box.

September 5

Dear Flora:

My first day of school was full of unlucky

situations **(2 points)**_____. I wanted to wear my favorite

shirt, but it was all rumpled **(2)**_____ from being

packed in a box. While I was looking for something else to

wear, I missed the bus. My parents drove me to school, but we

got lost on the way. We had to stop and ask for

directions **(2)**_____. I was worried **(2)**_____

that I would be late for school, but we got there just in time.

At noon, I couldn't find my lunchbox. I looked everywhere,

but it wasn't visible **(2)**_____. Then my day got

better. Some nice students asked me to sit with them. They

shared their lunches with me. It was an unusual **(2)**_____ way

to make new friends, but I'm glad it happened!

       Your friend,

       Joey

Theme 1: **Off to Adventure!**   47
Assessment Tip: Total **12** Points

Name _____

Event Map

Pages 94–95

Wendell and Floyd are at the principal's office. Then Mona

enters and says <u>she wants to look in the Lost and Found for her</u>

<u>lucky hat.</u> **(2 points)**

Page 96

Mona leans so far into the bin that only her feet are showing.

A moment later, <u>she disappears.</u> **(2)**

Pages 98–99

The boys <u>climb into the Lost and Found bin to find Mona.</u> **(2)**

Pages 102

The children see a sign to the Hat Room, so they follow a

passageway to <u>a cave, a lake, a suit of armor, and a boat.</u> **(2)**

Pages 104–106

The children come to a hallway lined with doors. Finally, Mona opens

one last door and finds <u>the Hat Room.</u> **(2)**

Assessment Tip: Total **10** Points

Name _____

Tell the True Story

The underlined part of each sentence below is false. Rewrite it as a true sentence about *The Lost and Found*.

1. Wendell and Floyd are waiting to see the principal because they missed <u>their bus</u>.

   Wendell and Floyd are waiting to see the principal because they

   missed a math test. **(2 points)**

2. Mona walks into the office to <u>borrow some lunch money</u>.

   Mona walks into the office to look for her lucky hat in the Lost

   and Found bin. **(2)**

3. The boys want to climb into the Lost and Found bin to <u>get away from a giant squid</u>.

   The boys want to climb into the Lost and Found bin to find

   Mona. **(2)**

4. The children cross the lake to find <u>the school library</u>.

   The children cross the lake to find the Hat Room and Mona's

   lucky hat. **(2)**

5. In the Hat Room, the boys start <u>looking for their lost baseball caps</u>.

   In the Hat Room, the boys start trying on hats to find lucky

   ones of their own. **(2)**

6. Mona finds her lucky hat <u>hanging on the Hat Room door</u>.

   Mona finds her lucky hat in her purse. **(2)**

Name _____

Story Events

Read the story. Think about what happens. Then fill in the chart on the next page.

Surprise!

After a long drive, Mom, Dad, and I got to Golden Lake. We were tired, so we set up camp and climbed into our sleeping bags. Then I said, "I hate camping. Why did you make me come?"

"You never know what can happen, Jenny," Dad answered. "You could be in for a big surprise!"

The next morning, I couldn't believe my eyes. There, sitting by the tent was a bee the size of an airplane! "Hop on!" shouted Dad over its loud hum. "Come for a ride."

We all got onto the bee's big, fuzzy back. Then it lifted off. It zoomed right and left. It sailed over the water and made loops in the air. What a fun ride!

At last, the bee landed by our camp. We all climbed off. Then it flew away. I stood there with my mouth open. Dad smiled and said, "Just wait until tomorrow's surprise!"

Name _____

The Lost and Found

Comprehension Skill
Sequence of Events

Story Events continued

Fill in the blanks to tell what happened in the story.

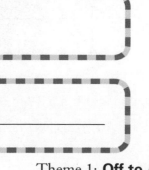

The family sets up camp at Golden Lake.

⬇

Jenny says she hates camping, but Dad tells her she may be in for a surprise.

⬇

The next morning _Jenny sees a bee as big as a plane._ **(2)**

⬇

The family climbs onto its back.

⬇

Then the bee _takes the family for a ride._ **(2)**

⬇

At last the bee _lands back at the campsite._ **(2)**

⬇

The family climbs off.

⬇

The bee _flies away._ **(2)**

Theme 1: **Off to Adventure!**   51
Assessment Tip: Total **8** Points

Name _____

Base Words

Some words are formed from a **base word,** a word that can stand by itself. In the word *climbing*, the base word is *climb*. Letters can be added to the beginning or the end of a base word, as you see here.

appear / **dis**appear   boat / boat**er**   turn / turn**ed**

Some of the words in this Lost and Found bin contain base words. Circle the base word in those words. Then write each base word on the lines below.

asked   unusual   closer   only
principal   trying   nonsense   loosely

1. _____ ask _____
2. _____ usual _____
3. _____ try _____
4. _____ close _____
5. _____ sense _____
6. _____ loose _____

Name _____

The Vowel-Consonant-*e* Pattern

The long *a, i, o,* and *u* sounds are shown as /ā/, /ī/, /ō/, and /o͞o/. When you hear these sounds, remember that they are often spelled with the vowel-consonant-*e* pattern.

   /ā/ s**a**ve   /ī/ l**i**fe   /ō/ sm**o**ke   /o͞o/ h**u**ge

► In the starred words *come* and *love*, the *o*-consonant-*e* pattern spells the /ŭ/ sound.

Write each Spelling Word under its vowel sound.
Order of answers for each category may vary.

Spelling Words

1. smoke
2. huge*
3. save
4. life
5. wide
6. come*
7. mine
8. grade
9. smile
10. note
11. cube
12. love

/ā/ or /ī/ Sound

save **(1 point)**

life **(1)**

wide **(1)**

mine **(1)**

grade **(1)**

smile **(1)**

/ō/ or /o͞o/ Sound

smoke **(1)**

huge **(1)**

note **(1)**

cube **(1)**

No long vowel Sound

come **(1)**

love **(1)**

Theme 1: **Off to Adventure!**   53
Assessment Tip: Total **12** Points

Name _____

Spelling Spree

Book Titles Write the Spelling Word that best completes each book title. Remember to use capital letters. (1 point each)

1. Sing Every <u>Note</u> by B. A. Soprano

2. I <u>Love</u> My Cats and Dogs by

   Ima Petowner

3. Dinosaurs Were <u>Huge</u>! by Sy N. Tific

4. Live Your <u>Life</u> to the Fullest by

   Hy Lee Adventurous

5. <u>Come</u> to My Party by U. R. Invited

Puzzle Play Write a Spelling Word for each clue. Then write the circled letters in order to spell something you might see over a waterfall.

6. a year of school g (r) a d e **(1)**

7. to keep for a while s (a) v e **(1)**

8. a happy expression s m (i) l e **(1)**

9. belongs to me m i (n) e **(1)**

10. one shape for ice c u (b) e **(1)**

11. fire can cause it s m (o) k e **(1)**

12. opposite of narrow (w) i d e **(1)**

  r a i n b o w

Name _____

Proofreading and Writing

Proofreading Circle the five misspelled Spelling Words in the sign. Then write each word correctly.

> ### MY HAT IS LOST!
> Please help me find my hat. I don't know where I left it. The hat is green and has a (wid) blue ribbon. My mother says it is (huje,) but I (luv) it. I'm sure no one else has a hat just like (min). If you find it, please leave a (not) on my locker.
> A classmate

Spelling Words
1. smoke
2. huge*
3. save
4. life
5. wide
6. come*
7. mine
8. grade
9. smile
10. note
11. cube
12. love

1. wide **(2 points)**

2. huge **(2)**

3. love **(2)**

4. mine **(2)**

5. note **(2)**

Write a Description Have you ever lost something that you liked very much, such as a piece of clothing or a toy?

On a separate sheet of paper, write a short description of the item you lost. Make sure to include details that would help someone recognize it. Use Spelling Words from the list. (2)

Responses will vary.

Name _____

Entry Words

Suppose Floyd wrote this letter. Decide whether each underlined word would be an entry word in a dictionary or part of an entry. Write the word in the correct column.

Dear Ms. Gernsblatt,

Our visit to the Lost and Found was a real <u>adventure</u>! First, Wendell and I <u>climbed</u> into the bin to find Mona. You cannot imagine what happened next. The bin became a deep well full of lost stuff. Mona was waiting for us at the bottom. We <u>followed</u> her into a cave. The cave had a treasure chest, a suit of <u>armor</u>, and a lot of other old things. We crossed a <u>bubbling</u> lake. We went through a <u>tunnel</u>. Then we came to a <u>winding</u> hallway. Finally, we found the Hat Room. You will not believe this, but Mona's hat was in her <u>purse</u> all along! After a long time, we found the way back. I think the three of us are going to be good friends.

Your student

Entry Word	**Part of an Entry**
adventure (**1 point**)	climbed (**1**)
armor (**1**)	followed (**1**)
tunnel (**1**)	bubbling (**1**)
purse (**1**)	winding (**1**)

Assessment Tip: Total **8** Points

Name _____

Finding Sentences

Read each group of words. Write *sentence* if the words are a complete sentence. Write *fragment* if the words are not a complete sentence. Then rewrite each fragment as a complete sentence. Add a word or words from the box at the bottom of the page.

Sentences for completed fragments will vary. Suggested sentences given.

1. Floyd wanted a hat. <u>sentence</u> **(2 points)**

   _____

2. Examined a suit of armor. <u>fragment</u> **(2)**

   <u>Wendell examined a suit of armor.</u>

3. The rumpled lucky hat. <u>fragment</u> **(2)**

   <u>The rumpled lucky hat disappeared.</u>

4. Mona looked for her missing hat. <u>sentence</u> **(2)**

   _____

5. Floated on the water. <u>fragment</u> **(2)**

   <u>The boat floated on the water.</u>

6. Flipped a coin. <u>fragment</u> **(2)**

   <u>Floyd flipped a coin.</u>

Word Bank

adventures	disappeared	Floyd
Mona	the boat	Wendell
worked		

Assessment Tip: Total **12** Points

Name _____

Changing Fragments to Sentences

Use each fragment below in a complete sentence.
Answers will vary. Suggested sentences given.

1. Floyd and his friend Wendell

   Floyd and his friend Wendell fought a giant squid. **(2 points)**

2. into a lost and found box

   Three friends dive into a lost and found box. **(2)**

3. loses her lucky hat

   Mona loses her lucky hat. **(2)**

4. looks like a dragon

   The boat looks like a dragon. **(2)**

5. in the hat room

   Floyd searches in the hat room. **(2)**

6. an exciting adventure in a strange world

   They go on an exciting adventure in a strange world. **(2)**

7. decides which cave to explore

   Wendell decides which cave to explore. **(2)**

8. a burgundy fez with a small gold tassel

   Wendell wears a burgundy fez with a small gold tassel. **(2)**

Assessment Tip: Total **16** Points

Name _____

Finding Sentences

Effective writers use complete sentences. Correct each sentence fragment. Write your revised sentence on each line. If it is a complete sentence, write the word *correct*.

Lucky Hats for Lucky Cats

1. Mona's cat. Likes Mona's lucky hat.

   Mona's cat likes Mona's lucky hat. **(2 points)**

2. Laughs at the ridiculous cat.

   Mona laughs at the ridiculous cat. **(2)**

3. The playful cat. Bites the floppy hat.

   The playful cat bites the floppy hat. **(2)**

4. Then the cat runs away with the hat.

   correct **(2)**

5. Chases her cat into the basement.

   Mona chases her cat into the basement. **(2)**

6. She hears. A meow.

   She hears a meow. **(2)**

7. Mona opens the suitcase.

   correct **(2)**

8. The cat. Is on her lucky hat.

   The cat is on her lucky hat. **(2)**

Assessment Tip: Total **16** Points

Name _____

Writing a Friendly Letter

The person I will write to: **(1 point)** _____

My address: _____

_____

The date: **(1)** _____

How I will greet the receiver: **(1)** _____

Why I want to write: **(1)** _____

_____

The most important thing I want to say: **(1)** _____

_____

_____

Important details I want to include: **(1)** _____

_____

_____

How I will close: **(1)** _____

_____

Assessment Tip: Total **8** Points

Name _____

Using Commas in Dates and Places

▶ When writing dates, use a comma between the day and the year.   **Example:** May 12, 2003

▶ Use a comma after the year except at the end of a sentence.

Example: On June 30, 2003, my sister will be ten years old.

▶ Use a comma between a town or city and the state.

Example: New Orleans, Louisiana

▶ Use a comma after the state except at the end of a sentence.

Example: My brother goes to college in New Orleans, Louisiana, and we will visit him next month.

Proofread the letter and add commas where necessary.

653 Cauterskill Road
(1 point) Catskills, New York 12414
(1) February 25, 2005

Dear Uncle Frank,

Our class is taking a field trip to New York City. Mom and Dad are going to be parent helpers. We want to spend an evening with you. We take a bus to New York, **(1)** New York, on May 12, 2005, and return on the morning of **(3)** May 14, 2005. Can you let us know right away which date **(1)** is best for you? We can't wait to see you in New York, **(1)** New York!

Your nephew,
Michael

Radio Words

**Fill each blank with the Key Vocabulary word that
best completes the sentence.**

1. Jake and Michael couldn't <u>raise **(1 point)**</u>

    their friend on the radio.

2. Is the radio <u>transmitting **(1)**</u> a signal?

3. High winds and rain from the

    <u>hurricane **(1)**</u> flooded the town and

    damaged many homes near the ocean.

4. Minutes before the show, the actor still couldn't find his

    costume. He was in great <u>distress **(1)**</u>.

5. There was a <u>ferocious **(1)**</u> snowstorm in January.

6. Marcus is in the principal's office. He is <u>relaying **(1)**</u>

    a message from his teacher.

Answer the questions.

7. Circle the two vocabulary words that have similar meanings.

    (relaying)   hurricane   distress   (transmitting)   **(2 points)**

8. Circle the animal that is the most ferocious.

    goldfish   rabbit   (lion)   mouse   **(2)**

Assessment Tip: Total **10** Points

Name _____

Cause-and-Effect Chart

**In each box, write a cause or an effect from the
appropriate story.** Answers may vary, but should reflect a cause and effect
relationship. Sample answers are given.

Radio Rescue

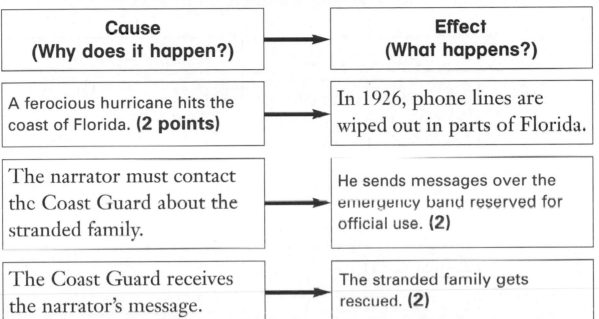

Cause (Why does it happen?)	Effect (What happens?)
A ferocious hurricane hits the coast of Florida. **(2 points)**	In 1926, phone lines are wiped out in parts of Florida.
The narrator must contact the Coast Guard about the stranded family.	He sends messages over the emergency band reserved for official use. **(2)**
The Coast Guard receives the narrator's message.	The stranded family gets rescued. **(2)**

Sybil Ludington's Midnight Ride

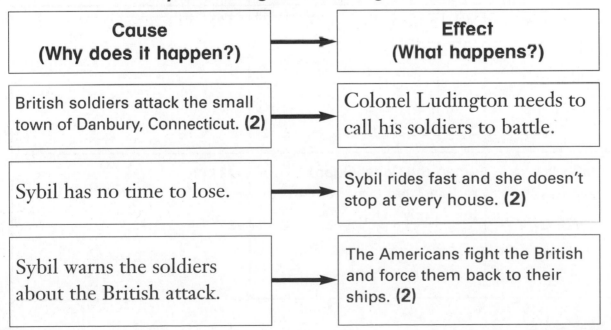

Cause (Why does it happen?)	Effect (What happens?)
British soldiers attack the small town of Danbury, Connecticut. **(2)**	Colonel Ludington needs to call his soldiers to battle.
Sybil has no time to lose.	Sybil rides fast and she doesn't stop at every house. **(2)**
Sybil warns the soldiers about the British attack.	The Americans fight the British and force them back to their ships. **(2)**

Assessment Tip: Total **12** Points

The High Point

The high point of a story is the point at which the story's events are most interesting and exciting. Complete the chart below to compare the high points of *Radio Rescue* and *Cliff Hanger.* Answers will vary. Sample answers provided.

	Radio Rescue	Cliff Hanger
What was the high point in the story?	when the boy was trying to send the message to the Coast Guard **(1 point)**	**(1)**
What kind of danger did someone in the story face?	A family was stranded on Key Largo. **(1)**	**(1)**
What did this part of the story make you wonder about?	Would the message get through? **(1)**	**(1)**
When did you know that the danger was over?	when the Coast Guard radioed that they had saved the family **(1)**	**(1)**

Assessment Tip: Total **8** Points

Name _____

Riders Beware!

Carousel is a friendly horse but there are certain things that upset him. Help the stable manager complete a sign that explains to riders how to keep Carousel happy.

Vocabulary

| reins | route | trot | urged |

My name is Carousel. I have lived at Sunshine

Stables for over 15 years. I know each

<u>route **(2 points)**</u> through the woods around here.

If you ride with me, you are in for a treat!

I like giving rides to people. I am usually very

friendly, but some things make me unfriendly.

I get angry when riders pull hard on my

<u>reins **(2)**</u>. It hurts my mouth.

I get mad when I am <u>urged **(2)**</u> to go fast.

I don't mind speeding up to a <u>trot **(2)**</u> now

and then, but I will not run!

If you follow my rules, I am sure we will get along

very well.

Name _____

Test Practice

Use the three steps you've learned to choose the best answer for these questions about *Sybil Ludington's Midnight Ride*. Fill in the circle next to the best answer.

1. Why does Sybil ride at night to the farms nearby? **(5 points)**

   ● She needs to tell the soldiers to gather at her father's farm.

   ○ She hopes to find shelter.

   ○ She wants to tell her father that the British are coming.

   ○ She must tell the soldiers to burn the town of Danbury.

2. Why did the author write this story? **(5)**

   ● to tell a story about an important event in history

   ○ to persuade readers to buy a horse like Star

   ○ to explain how to deliver an important message

   ○ to describe Sybil's childhood

3. Where does the story take place? **(5)**

   ○ in Great Britain   ○ on a farm

   ○ at Sybil's school   ● in Connecticut

4. **Connecting/Comparing** How is Sybil like Mulan in *The Ballad of Mulan?* **(5)**

   ○ She travels to faraway lands.

   ○ She misses her parents.

   ● She is brave during a war.

   ○ She hopes to become a general.

Continue on page 67.

Name _____

Test Practice *continued*

5. What is another good title for this story? **(5 points)**

   ○ Fires at Night

   ● Warning Soldiers

   ○ A Cold, Wet Ride

   ○ Sybil and Star

6. Why are the soldiers at their farms instead of with Colonel Ludington? **(5)**

   ○ They have decided not to fight the British.

   ● They have gone home to plant their crops.

   ○ They are hiding from the British.

   ○ They are gathering supplies for the fight.

7. How does Sybil probably feel when she hears the bell in Carmel? **(5)**

   ○ calm   ○ upset

   ○ worried   ● hopeful

8. **Connecting/Comparing** How are Sybil's actions similar to the boy's actions in *Radio Rescue?* **(5)**

   ○ She carefully writes down different names.

   ● She helps spread the word about an emergency.

   ○ She knows how to use a ham radio.

   ○ She tells family members that their loved ones are safe.

Name _____

What Happened? Why?

Read the information in the chart below. Then fill in the blanks to complete the chart. Look back at the Anthology pages listed if you want to check the details of an event.

Cause (Why did it happen?)	Effect (What happened?)
Sybil had no time to waste. **(2 points)** _____	Sybil stayed at each house just long enough to call out her message and listen for an answer. (page 132)
A cold rain was falling. (page 133)	Sybil's teeth chattered and her fingers felt stiff on the reins. **(2)** _____
Sybil saw fires burning in Danbury. (page 133)	Sybil thought about how she would feel if her own house were burning. **(2)**
Sybil knew that neighbors would run to tell one another. **(2)** _____	Sybil did not knock on every door. (page 134)
Sybil was able to warn the American soldiers about the British attacks. **(2)**	The American soldiers surprised the British and forced them back to their ships. (page 134)

68   Theme 1: **Off to Adventure!**
Assessment Tip: Total **10** Points

Name _____

When Did It Happen?

Read the paragraph.

Juana's clock radio turned on at 7 A.M. Juana groaned and rolled over, trying her best to ignore the radio announcer. A few minutes later, the announcer reported that a fire was burning at First and Main. First and Main? That was less than a block from Juana's house! Within seconds, Juana was out of bed, dressed, and looking out her window. She could see thick black smoke pouring from a window in Ms. Jaramelo's house. Juana scanned the street nervously. Just then, she spotted Ms. Jaramelo, safe and sound on the other side of the street. Moments later, Juana heard the sound of fire engine sirens.

Read the chart and fill in the blanks.

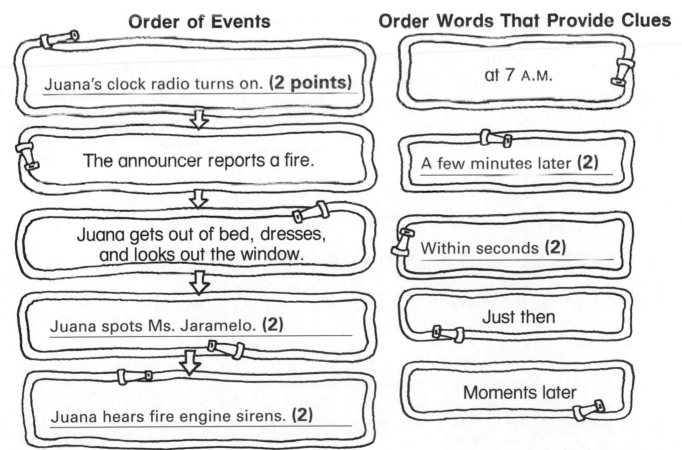

Order of Events

Juana's clock radio turns on. **(2 points)**

↓

The announcer reports a fire.

↓

Juana gets out of bed, dresses, and looks out the window.

↓

Juana spots Ms. Jaramelo. **(2)**

↓

Juana hears fire engine sirens. **(2)**

Order Words That Provide Clues

at 7 A.M.

A few minutes later **(2)**

Within seconds **(2)**

Just then

Moments later

Assessment Tip: Total **10** Points

Add an Ending

Complete each sentence with a word from the box. Use each word one time. Add *-ed* or *-ing* to the word so it makes sense in the sentence.

Remember:
- When a word ends in *e*, drop the *e* before adding *-ed* or *-ing*.
- When a word ends with a vowel and a consonant, double the consonant before adding *-ed* or *-ing*.

Word Bank

plan	come	hop	sail
arrive	like	run	stop

1. "Are you <u>planning **(1 point)**</u> to leave soon?" the radio operator asked.

2. "Our car is not <u>running **(1)**</u>," I said.

3. "Do you know a hurricane is <u>coming **(1)**</u>?" asked the operator.

4. "We heard the news and <u>hopped **(1)**</u> into our car."

5. "Then the car engine just <u>stopped **(1)**</u>."

6. "A Coast Guard ship is <u>sailing **(1)**</u> to your island," said the operator.

7. I <u>liked **(1)**</u> the sound of that news.

8. The ship <u>arrived **(1)**</u> at our house in less than an hour.

Name _____

Look for the Right Meaning

look *verb* **1.** To use the eyes to see: *I looked at the picture.* **2.** To focus one's gaze or attention: *Please look at the camera.* **3.** To appear; seem: *These bananas look ripe.* **4.** To search: *I looked everywhere for the missing key.* ♦ *noun* **1.** An act of looking: *I took a quick look at my watch.* **2.** An expression, as on a person's face: *She had a friendly look on her face.*

Read each sentence. Choose the correct definition of the underlined word. Write the definition on the line.

1. Dad and I <u>looked</u> for our binoculars.

   To search **(2 points)** _____

2. We wanted to <u>look</u> at the stars at night.

   To use the eyes to see **(2)** _____

3. The night sky <u>looks</u> so mysterious to me.

   To appear; seem **(2)** _____

4. I took a <u>look</u> through the binoculars.

   An act of looking **(2)** _____

5. When I saw them close up, the stars <u>looked</u> brighter.

   To appear; seem **(2)** _____

6. Dad said my face had an amazed <u>look</u>.

   An expression **(2)** _____

Assessment Tip: Total **12** Points

Name _____

Spelling Review

Write Spelling Words from the list to answer the questions. Order of answers in each category may vary.

1–17. Which seventeen words have short vowels?

1. drum **(1 point)**

2. last **(1)**

3. drop **(1)**

4. class **(1)**

5. left **(1)**

6. mix **(1)**

7. send **(1)**

8. smell **(1)**

9. stick **(1)**

10. thick **(1)**

11. hunt **(1)**

12. thin **(1)**

13. lot **(1)**

14. pond **(1)**

15. sock **(1)**

16. luck **(1)**

17. shut **(1)**

18–25. Which eight words have the vowel-consonant-*e* pattern?

18. huge **(1)**

19. wide **(1)**

20. save **(1)**

21. note **(1)**

22. grade **(1)**

23. cube **(1)**

24. life **(1)**

25. smile **(1)**

Spelling Words

1. drum
2. huge
3. last
4. drop
5. class
6. left
7. wide
8. mix
9. send
10. save
11. smell
12. stick
13. note
14. thick
15. hunt
16. thin
17. grade
18. lot
19. cube
20. pond
21. life
22. sock
23. luck
24. shut
25. smile

Assessment Tip: Total **25** Points

Name _____

Spelling Spree

Book Titles Write the Spelling Word that best completes each funny book title. Remember to use capital letters.

Spelling Words

1. class
2. mix
3. send
4. smell
5. stick
6. pond
7. sock
8. drum
9. huge
10. grade
11. cube
12. smile

Example: *The Great _____ from Planet X* by I. C. Starrs ___Escape___

1. *Put an Ice _____ in My Glass and Other Science Experiments* by Sy N. Seen

2. *A _____ Is a Frown Upside Down* by Mary Timz

3. *My First Day in _____ 3: A True Story* by Ima Newcomer

4. *The Mystery in the Third Grade _____* by Minnie Klooz

5. *_____ Us a Post Card* by U. R. A. Riter

6. *Do I _____ Cookies?* by I. M. Hungree

1. Cube **(1 point)**   4. Class **(1)**
2. Smile **(1)**   5. Send **(1)**
3. Grade **(1)**   6. Smell **(1)**

One, Two, Three! Write the Spelling Word that belongs in each group.

7. piano, guitar, drum **(1)**   10. stir, blend, mix **(1)**
8. big, large, huge **(1)**   11. shirt, shoe, sock **(1)**
9. lake, river, pond **(1)**   12. twig, branch, stick **(1)**

Name _____

Proofreading and Writing

Proofreading Circle the five misspelled Spelling Words below. Then write each word correctly.

January 12—Today I went on a treasure (hunte) I spent a (lott) of time looking for the treasure in a (thic) grove of trees and near the pond. I didn't have any (luk) Maybe somebody will (drap) a clue that I will find!

1. hunt **(1 point)**

2. lot **(1)**

3. thick **(1)**

4. luck **(1)**

5. drop **(1)**

	Spelling Words
1.	lot
2.	left
3.	thick
4.	life
5.	thin
6.	last
7.	luck
8.	note
9.	class
10.	hunt
11.	drop
12.	wide
13.	save
14.	shut

A Newspaper Article Write a Spelling Word that means the same as each underlined word or words.

Jeremy is a 6. <u>skinny</u> boy in Mr. Boyd's third grade 7. <u>group</u>. All of his 8. <u>years of being</u> Jeremy had heard about a buried treasure. One day he found a 9. <u>short letter</u> in his attic. It was all that was 10. <u>still around</u> of his grandfather's things. He 11. <u>closed</u> the door and read. "Keep your eyes 12. <u>all the way</u> open," it said. "Look under the 13. <u>final</u> tree in the yard." There Jeremy found a journal that he will 14. <u>keep</u>.

6. thin **(1 point)**

7. class **(1)**

8. life **(1)**

9. note **(1)**

10. left **(1)**

11. shut **(1)**

12. wide **(1)**

13. last **(1)**

14. save **(1)**

Write a Letter On a separate sheet of paper, write to a friend about a buried treasure you hope to find. Use the **Spelling Review Words.** Responses will vary. **(6)**

Assessment Tip: Total **20** Points

Finding Sentences

Read each group of words. Write *sentence* **if the words are a complete sentence. Write** *fragment* **if the words are not a complete sentence. Then rewrite each fragment as a complete sentence.** Sentences will vary. Suggested sentences given.

1. The boy listens to messages. sentence **(2 points)**

_____

2. Hears about a family in trouble. fragment **(1)**

   He hears about a family in trouble. **(1)**

3. Stranded on an island. fragment **(1)**

   The family is stranded on an island. **(1)**

4. He uses the emergency channel. sentence **(2)**

_____

5. Sends a message to the U.S. Coast Guard. fragment **(1)**

   The boy sends a message to the U. S. Coast Guard. **(1)**

6. The family has been saved! sentence **(2)**

_____

Assessment Tip: Total **12** Points

Name _____

Listing Subjects and Predicates

Write the complete subject of each sentence in the Subjects column. Write the complete predicate of each sentence in the Predicates column.

1. A young girl mounted her horse.

2. Rain fell from the sky.

3. The girl rode to a nearby farm.

4. She banged on the door.

5. A sleepy farmer opened the door.

6. The young rider shouted the news.

Subjects	Predicates
A young girl **(1 point)**	mounted her horse. **(1)**
Rain **(1)**	fell from the sky. **(1)**
The girl **(1)**	rode to a nearby farm. **(1)**
She **(1)**	banged on the door. **(1)**
A sleepy farmer **(1)**	opened the door. **(1)**
The young rider **(1)**	shouted the news. **(1)**

Assessment Tip: Total **12** Points

Name _____

Poetry Words

Choose the word from the box that best completes each sentence. Then circle each word in the puzzle below.

Vocabulary

> **Vocabulary**
>
> beats
> lines
> pattern
> rhyme
> rhythm
> stanzas

1. *Night, write,* and *sight* are words that ___rhyme__ **(2 points)** .

2. The first two __lines__ **(2)** of my poem have six words each.

3. I counted the __beats__ **(2)** in every line.

4. The __pattern__ **(2)** of the rhymes is that every pair of lines rhyme.

5. My poem is divided into four __stanzas__ **(2)** . Each one has four lines.

6. My poem has a gentle, steady __rhythm__ **(2)** .

R	H	Y	M	L	P	L	P	S	B
H	E	S	B	I	B	I	A	T	R
Y	S	T	E	N	E	N	T	A	H
T	R	P	A	T	T	E	R	N	Y
H	H	S	T	A	N	S	H	Z	M
M	Y	P	S	T	A	N	R	A	S
P	A	T	R	H	Y	M	E	S	L

Assessment Tip: Total **12** Points

Name _____

Patterns of Poetry
Answers will vary. Sample answers are given.

Poems with Rhyme Words

Poem	Poem	Poem
"Sneeze"	"Joe"	"Cloud Dragons"
Pairs of Rhyme Words	**Pairs of Rhyme Words**	**Pairs of Rhyme Words**
nickel/prickle **(2 points)**	seeds/breeds **(2)**	do/blue **(2)**

Poems with Repeated Words

Poem	Poem	Poem
"April Rain Song"	"Cloud Dragons"	"Spaghetti! Spaghetti!"
Examples of Repeated Words	**Examples of Repeated Words**	**Examples of Repeated Words**
"Let the rain," "The rain" **(2)**	"What do you see / in the clouds so high?" **(2)**	"Spaghetti! Spaghetti!" **(2)**

Poems with Different Line Patterns

Poems with Very Short Lines	Poems Written in Stanzas	Poems with Lines That Form a Shape
"Sneeze," If I Were an Ant," "Books" **(2)**	"April Rain Song," "Cloud Dragons," "Spaghetti! Spaghetti!" "Andre," "Books" **(2)**	"Giraffe" **(2)**

Assessment Tip: Total **18** Points

Name ______________________________

Comparing Poems

Think about the elements of poetry. Choose three poems to compare and contrast. Then complete the chart below.
Answers will vary.

	Title: ______	Title: ______	Title: ______
What picture does the poem create in your mind?	(2 points)	(2)	(2)
What feeling does the poem express?	(2)	(2)	(2)
What kind of language is used in each poem?	(2)	(2)	(2)

Tell which of these poems is your favorite and why. **(2)**

Answers will vary.

Assessment Tip: Total **20** Points

Name _____

And the Winner Is ....

You are presenting the annual Poetry Prizes. Below are the notes for your speech. Use the poems from this theme to fill in the blanks. Answers may vary.

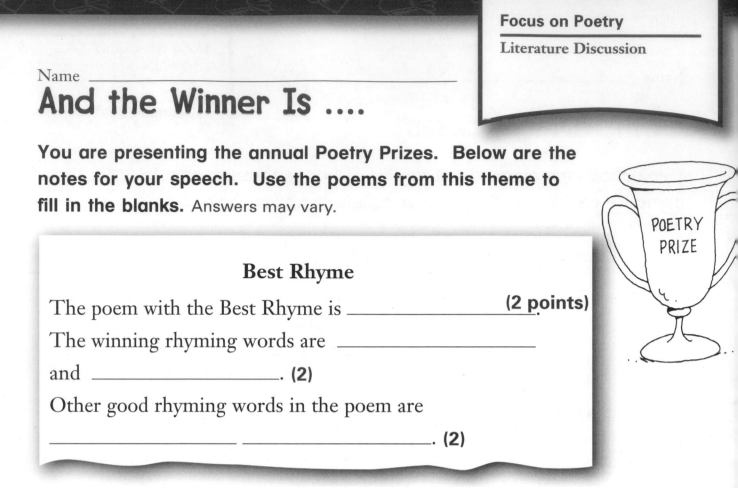

Best Rhyme

The poem with the Best Rhyme is _____. **(2 points)**

The winning rhyming words are _____

and _____. **(2)**

Other good rhyming words in the poem are

_____ _____. **(2)**

Best Rhythm

The poem with the Best Rhythm is _____. **(2)**

A line I like from the poem is _____ **(2)**

_____.

Best Words That Paint a Picture

The poem with the Best Words That Paint a Picture

is _____. **(2)**

My favorite lines from the poem are _____ **(2)**

_____

_____.

Assessment Tip: Total **14** Points

Name _____

Tell About a Poem

Choose another poem to study closely. Make notes about rhyme words, images, and repetition on the chart. Then write a paragraph that describes how the poem uses each of these elements. Use examples to support your ideas.

Answers will vary.

Poem: _____

Rhyme Words	
Images	
Repetition	

_____

_____

_____

_____

_____

_____

Focus on Poetry

Structural Analysis Prefixes
un-, *dis-*, and *non-*; Suffixes
-y and *-ly*

Good Muffin, Healthy Muffin

Some words combine a prefix and a base word.

    un- + true untrue

    dis- + appear disappear

    non- + stop   nonstop

Other words combine a base word and a suffix.

    mess + -y messy

    slow + -ly slowly

Some words combine a prefix, a base word, and a suffix.

    un- + fair + -ly   unfairly

Read this poem. Circle each word that has a prefix or suffix shown in the chart. Write each word and its base word to complete the chart.

I buy a (nonfat) muffin.
It looks (sugary) and sweet.
And when I (quickly) take a bite,
I find that it's a treat!

I don't (dislike) my muffin
Although I thought I would.
It's not at all (unpleasant,)
It's (healthy) and it's good!

Word with Prefix or Suffix	Base Word
un-	
unpleasant **(1 point)**	pleasant **(1)**
dis-	
dislike **(1)**	like **(1)**
non-	
nonfat **(1)**	fat **(1)**
-y	
sugary **(1)**	sugar **(1)**
healthy **(1)**	health **(1)**
-ly	
quickly **(1)**	quick **(1)**

Assessment Tip: Total **12** Points

Name _____

More Short and Long Vowels

A short vowel sound is often spelled with one vowel followed by a consonant sound.

     st**a**nd   tw**i**st

A long vowel sound is often spelled vowel-consonant-e.

     pl**ate**   wh**ite**

Write each Spelling Word under the heading that describes its vowel sound.

Order of words in each column may vary.

<table>
<tr><th>Short Vowel Sound</th><th>Long Vowel Sound</th></tr>
<tr><td>stand (1 point)</td><td>plate (1)</td></tr>
<tr><td>rest (1)</td><td>white (1)</td></tr>
<tr><td>clock (1)</td><td>frame (1)</td></tr>
<tr><td>stuff (1)</td><td>spoke (1)</td></tr>
<tr><td>bend (1)</td><td>June (1)</td></tr>
<tr><td>twist (1)</td><td>mile (1)</td></tr>
</table>

Spelling Words

1. stand
2. rest
3. plate
4. clock
5. white
6. stuff
7. spoke
8. bend
9. frame
10. twist
11. June
12. mile

Assessment Tip: Total **12** Points

Name _____

Spelling Spree

**Rhyme Time Fill in the blank in each sentence with a
Spelling Word that rhymes with the underlined word.**

1. stand
2. rest
3. plate
4. clock
5. white
6. stuff
7. spoke
8. bend
9. frame
10. twist
11. June
12. mile

1. The strong man could __stand **(1 point)**__ on one
   <u>hand</u>.

2. Did you __twist **(1)**__ your <u>wrist</u> when you
   fell down?

3. That <u>block</u> is painted to look like a
   __clock **(1)**__.

4. Mia's new <u>kite</u> looks like a __white **(1)**__ bird.

5. When Dan __spoke **(1)**__, he told a funny <u>joke</u>.

6. To do well on the <u>test</u>, you need plenty of
   __rest **(1)**__.

**Letter Swap Change the underlined letter in each word to
make a Spelling Word. Then write the Spelling Word.**

7. mi<u>n</u>e __mile **(1)**__

8. <u>m</u>end __bend **(1)**__

9. pla<u>n</u>e __plate **(1)**__

10. <u>t</u>une __June **(1)**__

11. <u>f</u>lame __frame **(1)**__

12. sti<u>f</u>f __stuff **(1)**__

Assessment Tip: Total **12** Points

Name _____

Proofreading and Writing

Proofreading Circle the four misspelled Spelling
Words in this poem. Then write each word correctly.

Order of answers may vary.

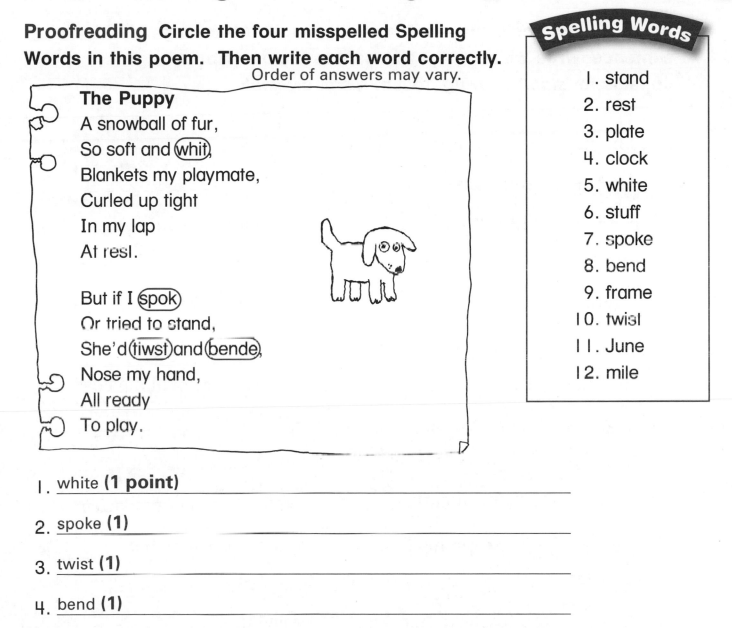

The Puppy

A snowball of fur,

So soft and (whit),

Blankets my playmate,

Curled up tight

In my lap

At resl.

But if I (spok)

Or tried to stand,

She'd (tiwst) and (bende),

Nose my hand,

All ready

To play.

Spelling Words

1. stand
2. rest
3. plate
4. clock
5. white
6. stuff
7. spoke
8. bend
9. frame
10. twist
11. June
12. mile

1. white **(1 point)**

2. spoke **(1)**

3. twist **(1)**

4. bend **(1)**

Write a Poem About an Animal Do you have a pet or a
favorite animal? What does it look like? How does it act?
Why do you love or like it?

**On a separate piece of paper, write a poem about a pet or
your favorite animal. Use Spelling Words from the list.**

Poems will vary. **(4)**

Assessment Tip: Total **8** Points

Name _____

Use Your Senses

Each sentence below uses sensory language. After each sentence, write which of the five senses the description appeals to: *sight, hearing, touch, taste,* **or** *smell.*

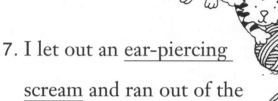

1. The tiny kitten was as <u>soft as a dandelion</u> in the palm of my hand. <u>touch **(1 point)**</u>

2. His long fur was as <u>golden as autumn leaves.</u>
   <u>sight **(1)**</u>

3. He licked my arm with his <u>sandpaper-rough tongue.</u>
   <u>touch **(1)**</u>

4. I noticed his <u>sweet, slightly fishy breath</u> as he purred in my face.
   <u>smell **(1)**</u>

5. "What a sweet kitty!" I said in a <u>syrupy voice.</u> <u>hearing **(1)**</u>

6. I was startled when his <u>knife-sharp claws</u> sank into my arm.
   <u>touch **(1)**</u>

7. I let out an <u>ear-piercing scream</u> and ran out of the room. <u>hearing **(1)**</u>

8. A glass of <u>refreshingly cold water</u> calmed me down.
   <u>taste **(1)**</u>

9. When I went back into the living room, the kitten gazed at me with his <u>sorrowful emerald eyes.</u>
   <u>sight **(1)**</u>

10. I said, "Oh, okay, I forgive you," and I poured him a bowl of <u>rich, delicious cream.</u>
    <u>taste **(1)**</u>

Assessment Tip: Total **10** Points

Name _____

Matching Sentence Parts

Choose a subject or a predicate from the lists below to complete each fragment. Write the complete sentence on the line. Some subjects and predicates will not be used.

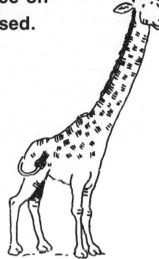

Subjects	Predicates
the tall giraffe	hung upside down
spaghetti with sauce	curled their tails
the shimmering blue sky	ran across the picnic table
Andre	gobbled his dinner
the birds on the feeder	beat upon my head

Answers may vary. Sample answers are given.

1. Is delicious to eat.

   Spaghetti with sauce is delicious to eat. **(2 points)**

2. The April rain

   The April rain beat upon my head. **(2)**

3. Dreamed about his parents.

   Andre dreamed about his parents. **(2)**

4. Walked around on wooden stilts.

   The tall giraffe walked around on wooden stilts. **(2)**

5. The batty bat.

   The batty bat hung upside down. **(2)**

6. Tiny red ants.

   Tiny red ants ran across the picnic table. **(2)**

Name _____

Correcting Fragments

**Read the paragraph. Correct each sentence fragment, and
write the revised paragraph below.**
Answers may vary. Sample answers are given.

I wrote. A funny poem. It told about a silly dragon.
The dragon. Sneezed. A lot. One sneeze made a house
fall down. One made a tree crash. Into a pond. The
poor dragon felt sad. He asked a friendly dog. For help.
The dog gave this advice. He told the dragon to eat his
food. With less pepper. The dragon's problem. Went away.
Now he sneezed. A lot less. And felt better.

_____I wrote a funny poem. **(2 points)** It told about a silly dragon._____

The dragon sneezed a lot. **(3)** One sneeze made a house fall down.

One made a tree crash into a pond. **(2)** The poor dragon felt sad.

He asked a friendly dog for help. **(2)** The dog gave this advice.

He told the dragon to eat his food with less pepper. **(2)** The dragon's

problem went away. **(2)** Now he sneezed a lot less and felt better. **(3)**

Assessment Tip: Total **16** Points

Name _____

Sentence Punctuation and Capitalization

Use proofreading marks to correct six missing or incorrect end marks and four missing capital letters in this paragraph from a poet's writing diary.

1 point for each correction

Example:

the songs of the birds woke me at five o'clock today.

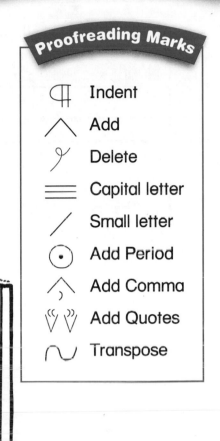

Saturday

 what a wonderful morning it is. My sister

and I took a long walk in the park. my sister

found a baby bird on the ground. We sat and

watched it. the bird stayed very still. At last

it shook its feathers and flew away. did its

tiny wings carry it to a safe place. I must

write a poem about this beautiful little bird.

Name _____

Writing a Shape Poem

Topic _Answers will vary. **(2 points)**_____

Nouns	Verbs	The Five Senses
Answers will vary. **(2)**	**(2)**	**(2)**

Organizing the Words in a Shape

(4)

Assessment Tip: Total 12 Points

Name _____

Cool Cat Nouns

Help this poet who wants to write a shape poem about a cat. Find six exact nouns that tell about cats. Write them on the lines below.

old	run	soft	hand
paw	tail	claw	nose
bark	silly	whiskers	happy
fur	elephant	sleepy	fork

Exact Nouns Order of answers may vary.

1. paw **(2 points)**

2. fur **(2)**

3. tail **(2)**

4. claw **(2)**

5. whiskers **(2)**

6. nose **(2)**

Assessment Tip: Total **12** Points

Name _____

Celebrating Traditions

Describe a tradition that you celebrate. When do you celebrate it? Who shares the celebration with you? What is your favorite part of this tradition? (5 points)

_____

_____

_____

_____

_____

_____

_____

List any traditions you would like to learn about.

(5) _____

_____

_____

_____

Name _____

Celebrating Traditions

Fill in the chart as you read the stories. Sample answers shown.

The Keeping Quilt

What tradition is celebrated in this selection?
Polacco celebrates family events by using a quilt that is passed down from generation to generation. **(2 points)**

Why is this tradition important to those who celebrate it?
Polacco's quilt reminds her of the difficult and wonderful events that have happened in her family over the years. **(3)**

Grandma's Records

What tradition is celebrated in this selection?
The boy spends every summer at his grandmother's apartment. **(2)**

Why is this tradition important to those who celebrate it?
The boy learns to appreciate the music that his grandmother shares with him, and Grandma also learns to enjoy the new music her grandson plays for her. **(3)**

The Talking Cloth

What tradition is celebrated in this selection?
Amber learns about the printed cloth that celebrates her heritage and how it can express the character of different family members. **(2)**

Why is this tradition important to those who celebrate it?
The Talking Cloth allows Amber to learn more about herself, her history, and the other people in her family. **(3)**

Dancing Rainbows

What tradition is celebrated in this selection?
Curt learns about the dancing traditions of his ancestors. **(2)**

Why is this tradition important to those who celebrate it?
Curt learns about his ancestors and gets to spend time with his grandfather. **(3)**

Assessment Tip: Total **20** Points

Name _____

Quilt Crossword

Write the word that matches each clue in
the puzzle. Use the vocabulary words for help.

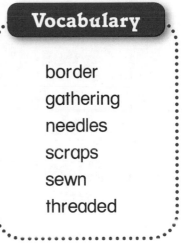

Crossword grid:

Across: ¹g a t h e r i n g (down), ²s c r a p s (down), ³t h r e a d e d (down), ⁴b o r d e r (across), ⁵s e w n (down), ⁶n e e d l e s (across)

Vocabulary

border
gathering
needles
scraps
sewn
threaded

Across

4. edge **(2 points)**

6. tools for sewing **(2)**

Down

1. coming together **(2)**

2. leftover pieces **(2)**

3. passed through the eye
   of a needle **(2)**

5. put together with a
   needle and thread **(2)**

Name _____

Author's Family Chart
Accept varied responses.

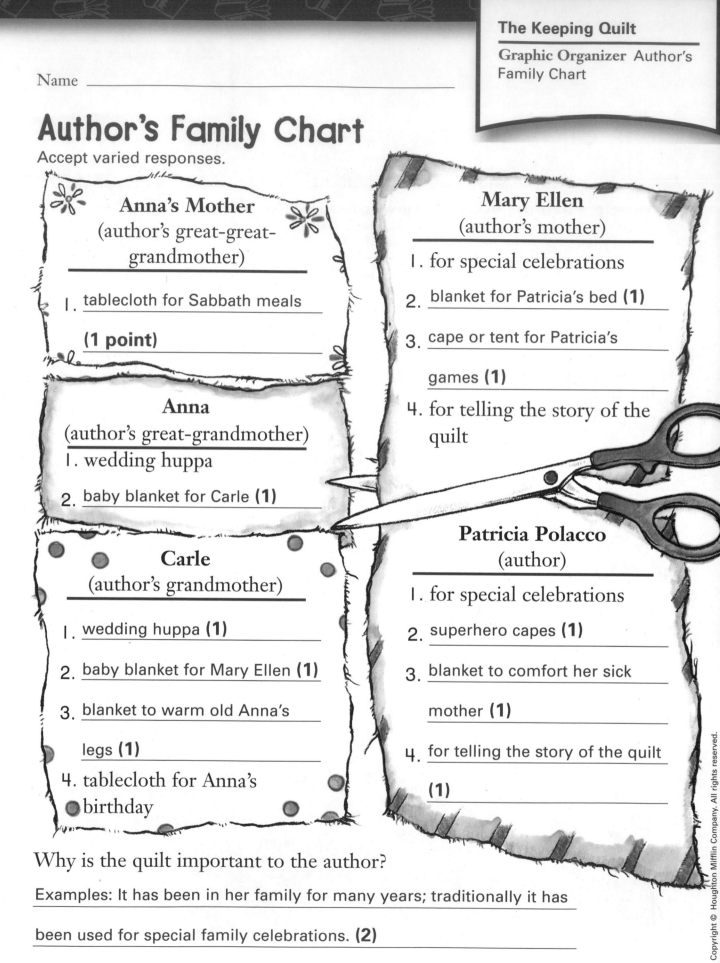

Anna's Mother
(author's great-great-grandmother)

1. tablecloth for Sabbath meals

(1 point)

Anna
(author's great-grandmother)
1. wedding huppa
2. baby blanket for Carle **(1)**

Carle
(author's grandmother)

1. wedding huppa **(1)**

2. baby blanket for Mary Ellen **(1)**

3. blanket to warm old Anna's

legs **(1)**

4. tablecloth for Anna's birthday

Mary Ellen
(author's mother)

1. for special celebrations

2. blanket for Patricia's bed **(1)**

3. cape or tent for Patricia's

games **(1)**

4. for telling the story of the quilt

Patricia Polacco
(author)

1. for special celebrations

2. superhero capes **(1)**

3. blanket to comfort her sick

mother **(1)**

4. for telling the story of the quilt

(1)

Why is the quilt important to the author?

Examples: It has been in her family for many years; traditionally it has

been used for special family celebrations. **(2)**

96   Theme 2: **Celebrating Traditions**
Assessment Tip: Total **12** Points

Name _____

Piece It Together

Finish each statement with details from *The Keeping Quilt*.
Answers may vary. Examples are given.

1. Anna's mother decides to make the quilt because

   it will be a good way to remember the home and family they left in

   Russia. **(2 points)**

2. When Carle grows up, Great-Gramma Anna passes
   the quilt on to her. She

   uses it and passes it on to Mary Ellen, her daughter. **(2)**

3. Over the years, people in the family use the quilt as

   a wedding huppa, a baby blanket, a pretend cape, and a tablecloth

   for celebrations. **(2)**

4. Mary Ellen tells her daughter (the author) whose

   clothes were used to make the quilt. **(2)**

5. Mary Ellen also is lucky enough to tell the story of the quilt to

   her grandchildren and great-grandchildren. **(2)**

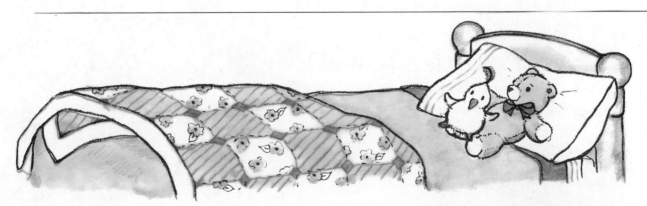

Name _____

An Author's View

Read the story. Then finish the chart on the next page.

Foxtails

When I first saw Grandma Sorensen in her doorway, she seemed ten feet tall and skinny! She frowned as she squinted into the sun and watched our car. Would I like her?

In the living room, Grandma Sorensen gave each of us a big hug. Then she and Mom began talking. Soon they were laughing about things Mom did as a girl. Once she fell out of their apple tree and broke her arm. Then Grandma told how she too had fallen out of an apple tree and broken her arm. That was when she was a girl in Denmark. I said, "I'm never going to climb apple trees!" Grandma laughed.

Later, after Mom had left for a meeting, Grandma suggested that we make my mother a treat, the one she loved best at my age. In the kitchen, Grandma let me mix flour, sugar, eggs, butter, and vanilla together to make a stiff dough. Then she showed me how to pinch off a small piece of dough, roll it, and twist it into a "foxtail." She didn't mind that I made the tails a bit crooked.

As we worked, Grandma asked me about school and what I wanted to be when I grew up. From her questions I could tell she was really interested in what I said. What a good listener! By the time Mom returned, the foxtails were ready to eat, and Grandma and I were best friends.

Name _____

An Author's View continued

Use story details to finish this chart. Tell how the author feels about her grandmother. Answers may vary.

Scene	Details About Grandma	Author's Feelings About Grandma
The Doorway	1. She seems ten feet tall. **(1 point)** 2. She frowns as she watches the car. **(1)**	She seems big and scary. **(1)**
The Living Room	1. She happily remembers tales from the past. **(1)** 2. She laughs often. **(1)**	She enjoys remembering the past. **(1)**
The Kitchen	1. She lets the author make foxtails. **(1)** 2. She's really interested in what the author says. **(1)**	She's patient and a good listener. **(1)**

If you met Grandma Sorensen, do you think you would like her? Why or why not? Use complete sentences.

Answers may vary.

_____

_____

Name _____

Compound Mix-up

Write a compound word to match each picture clue.
Each word is made up of two words from the Word Bank.

Word Bank

dog	bug	pot	lady	flower	flag
fly	dragon	tooth	rain	fish	bow
house	brush	pole	moon	star	light

dragonfly **(1 point)**

doghouse **(1)**

flagpole **(1)**

toothbrush **(1)**

ladybug **(1)**

starfish **(1)**

moonlight **(1)**

rainbow **(1)**

flowerpot **(1)**

Combine two words from the Word Bank to make a new compound word. Answers will vary.

(1) _____

Assessment Tip: Total **10** Points

Name _____

More Long Vowel Spellings

To spell a word with the /ā/ sound, remember that /ā/ can be spelled *ai* or *ay*. To spell a word with the /ē/ sound, remember that /ē/ can be spelled *ea* or *ee*.

| /ā/ | ai, ay | p**ai**nt, cl**ay** |
| /ē/ | ea, ee | l**ea**ve, f**ee**l |

► In the starred words *neighbor, eight,* and *weigh,* the /ā/ sound is spelled *eigh*.

Write each Spelling Word under its vowel sound.
Order of answers for each category may vary.

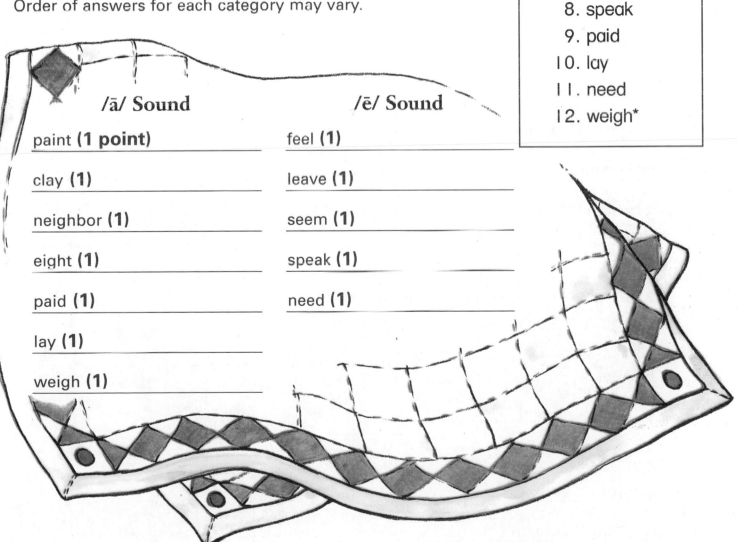

/ā/ Sound

paint **(1 point)**

clay **(1)**

neighbor **(1)**

eight **(1)**

paid **(1)**

lay **(1)**

weigh **(1)**

/ē/ Sound

feel **(1)**

leave **(1)**

seem **(1)**

speak **(1)**

need **(1)**

Name _____

Spelling Spree

Fill in the Blank Write the Spelling Word that best completes each sentence.

1. I whisper when I need to _____ softly.

2. My _____ lives across the street.

3. I stand on the scale when I want to _____ myself.

4. My brother formed a bowl out of _____.

5. I set up my easel when I want to _____.

6. One more than seven is _____.

7. I don't want to stay, so I will _____.

Spelling Words

1. paint
2. clay
3. feel
4. leave
5. neighbor*
6. eight*
7. seem
8. speak
9. paid
10. lay
11. need
12. weigh*

1. <u>speak **(1 point)**</u>   5. <u>paint **(1)**</u>

2. <u>neighbor **(1)**</u>   6. <u>eight **(1)**</u>

3. <u>weigh **(1)**</u>   7. <u>leave **(1)**</u>

4. <u>clay **(1)**</u>

Letter Swap Write a Spelling Word by changing the first letter of each word.

8. peel   <u>feel **(1)**</u>

9. maid   <u>paid **(1)**</u>

10. seed   <u>need **(1)**</u>

11. say   <u>lay **(1)**</u>

12. teem   <u>seem **(1)**</u>

Assessment Tip: Total **12** Points

Name _____

Proofreading and Writing

Proofreading Circle the five misspelled Spelling
Words in this invitation. Then write each word
correctly.

Spelling Words

1. paint
2. clay
3. feel
4. leave
5. neighbor*
6. eight*
7. seem
8. speak
9. paid
10. lay
11. need
12. weigh*

Dear New Neighbor,

Please join me and some of the other tenants in
the building for a quilting party. I have enough
needles and thread for (eaght) helpers. You don't (ned)
to be a sewing expert. The work will (seam) easy, and
we will all get to know one another. Later we will
have tea and cake. The party will be in my
apartment next Monday evening. If you are
interested, (spek) to me soon. If you prefer, you can
(leve) a note in my mailbox instead.

Sincerely,
Natasha Pushkin

1. eight **(2 points)** _____

2. need **(2)** _____

3. seem **(2)** _____

4. speak **(2)** _____

5. leave **(2)** _____

Write a Description If you were going to design a quilt
like the one in the story, what would it look like?

**On a separate sheet of paper, write about a quilt you would
design. Tell what material you would use and why. Use
Spelling Words from the list.** Responses will vary. **(2)**

Name _____

Word Family Reunion

Select the words that belong to the word family for "back."
Then arrange the words on the chart and define each one.
Check your work in a dictionary.

Word Bank

backward	bacteria	backyard	bachelor	backboard
backbone	backfire	background	backpack	backup

The Back Family

Word	Meaning
1. backward **(1 point)**	in the opposite direction **(1)**
2. backyard **(1)**	yard at the back of the house **(1)**
3. backboard **(1)**	flat board used in basketball **(1)**
4. backbone **(1)**	the spine **(1)**
5. backfire **(1)**	to have a bad or unexpected result **(1)**
6. background **(1)**	part of the scene not in the front **(1)**
7. backpack **(1)**	bag worn on the back **(1)**
8. backup **(1)**	support or help **(1)**

Assessment Tip: Total **16** Points

Name _____

In Search of Common Nouns

Circle the common noun or nouns in each group of words.

1. big (room) **(1)**

2. (quilt) sewed (needle) **(1)**

3. (house) talk enjoy (people) **(1)**

4. (blanket) warm (sister) (friend) **(1)**

5. happy silly (story) angry **(1)**

6. curious (city) cheerful sad **(1)**

Write the circled nouns in the correct square below.

Persons

people **(1 point)**

sister **(1)**

friend **(1)**

Things

quilt **(1)**

needle **(1)**

blanket **(1)**

story **(1)**

Places

room **(1)**

house **(1)**

city **(1)**

Name _____

Common Nouns in Signs

Find the common nouns in the report. Write each common noun in the correct exhibit room below.

A Visit to the Museum

My friends and I visited a museum. There we saw a collection of wonderful old quilts. Some of them were made by pioneers. Many of the blankets showed children, flowers, and trees. One showed all fifty states.

Exhibit Room 1: People

friends **(1 point)** _____

pioneers **(1)** _____

children **(1)** _____

Exhibit Room 2: Places

museum **(1)** _____

states **(1)** _____

Exhibit Room 3: Things

collection **(1)** _____

quilts **(1)** _____

blankets **(1)** _____

flowers **(1)** _____

trees **(1)** _____

Assessment Tip: Total **10** Points

Name _____

Commas in a Series

Proofread each sentence. Add commas to separate each series of three or more words. Remove all unnecessary commas.

1. Our attic is filled with boxes bags and books.

   Our attic is filled with boxes, bags, and books. **(1 point)**

2. I found my great-grandfather's hat gloves and cane.

   I found my great-grandfather's hat, gloves, and cane. **(1)**

3. The cane was carved with tigers lions and elephants.

   The cane was carved with tigers, lions, and elephants. **(1)**

4. I also found old journals photographs and drawings.

   I also found old journals, photographs, and drawings. **(1)**

5. One photograph shows my aunt uncle and cousin.

   One photograph shows my aunt, uncle, and cousin. **(1)**

6. My great-grandmother lived on a farm with chickens cows horses and pigs.

   My great-grandmother lived on a farm with chickens, cows,

   horses, and pigs. **(1)**

7. In her diary, she described her, friends relatives and visitors.

   In her diary, she described her friends, relatives, and visitors. **(1)**

8. Her hopes wishes and dreams, bring every page to life.

   Her hopes, wishes, and dreams bring every page to life. **(1)**

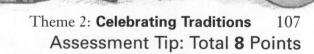

Name _____

Paragraphs That Compare and Contrast

Use the chart on this page to help you plan paragraphs that compare and contrast. Write what the paragraphs will be about. Write two or three interesting details that show how the people, places, and things are alike. Then write how they are different. Use the details you record in your writing.

What I Will Compare and Contrast

(Answers will vary.) _____

_____

How They Are Alike	How They Are Different
1. **(1 point)** _____ _____	1. **(1)** _____ _____
2. **(1)** _____ _____	2. **(1)** _____ _____
3. **(1)** _____	3. **(1)** _____

Write your paragraphs that compare and contrast on a separate sheet of paper. Include the details you wrote above. **(4 points)**

Assessment Tip: Total **10** Points

Name _____

Sentence Combining

▶ Connect two related sentences with a comma and a joining word to make a compound sentence.

▶ Use a comma and the word *and* to create a compound sentence that makes a comparison.

> **Example:** The gifts were part of the women's bouquets, **and** each gift was a symbol of something important for a good life.

▶ Use a comma and the word *but* to create a compound sentence that makes a contrast.

> **Example:** At the first weddings, the women wore wedding dresses, **but** later some women wore suits.

Write a compound sentence. Combine the sentences with a comma and the joining word in parentheses ( ).

1. The women loved the keeping quilt. They used it to keep their family's traditions alive. (and)

   The women loved the keeping quilt, and they used it to keep their

   family's traditions alive. **(2 points)**

2. The women's weddings were alike in some ways. They were also different. (but)

   The women's weddings were alike in some ways,

   but they were also different. **(2)**

3. The quilt was used as a cape. It was used as a huppa too. (and)

   The quilt was used as a cape, and it was used as a huppa too. **(2)**

Name _____

Revising Your Instructions

Reread your instructions. Put a checkmark in the box for each sentence that describes your paper. Use this page to help you revise.

Rings the Bell

☐ An interesting beginning tells my topic.

☐ I included all the necessary materials, steps, and details.

☐ The steps are told in order, using time-order words.

☐ I used many exact words. My writing sounds interesting.

☐ Sentences flow well. There are no mistakes.

Getting Stronger

☐ The beginning tells about my topic but isn't interesting.

☐ I forgot a step or some materials. More details are needed.

☐ A step might be out of order. I used few time-order words.

☐ More exact words are needed. My voice could be stronger.

☐ Some sentences are choppy. There are a few mistakes.

Try Harder

☐ The beginning is missing or doesn't tell my topic.

☐ Many steps are missing. There are almost no details.

☐ The steps are not in order. The instructions are confusing.

☐ There are no exact words. I can't hear my voice at all.

☐ Most sentences are choppy. Mistakes make it hard to read.

Name _____

Using Exact Nouns

**Circle the letter of the noun that best replaces each
underlined word or phrase.**

1. Do you want to be a movie <u>person who acts</u>?

   a. lawyer   b. watcher   c. star **(1 point)**   d. Venus

2. First, you need to have a good head of <u>fuzzy stuff</u>.

   a. hair **(1)**   b. ears   c. smile   d. connections

3. Then, you need some cool clothes and a pair of
   dark <u>eye things</u>.

   a. pupils   b. carrots   c. cups   d. sunglasses **(1)**

4. Next, you need a big, fancy house with a <u>big thing of water</u>.

   a. garage   b. door   c. pool **(1)**   d. yard

5. You'll need to eat at all the best eating <u>places</u>.

   a. restaurants **(1)** b. stations   c. rinks   d. garages

6. Of course, you need to have an agent and a <u>person who
   represents you legally</u>.

   a. judge   b. sheriff   c. lawyer **(1)**   d. partner

7. Do you need any actual acting <u>stuff</u>?

   a. manners   b. talent **(1)**   c. rules   d. clothes

8. "It helps, but it's not a must," say all the top Hollywood movie <u>leaders</u>.

   a. sleepers   b. sellers   c. drivers   d. directors **(1)**

Theme 2: **Celebrating Traditions**   111
Assessment Tip: Total **8** Points

Name _____

Spelling Words

Look for spelling patterns you have learned to help you remember the Spelling Words on this page. Think about the parts that you find hard to spell.

Write the missing letters and apostrophe in the Spelling Words below.

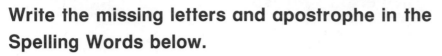

Spelling Words

1. now
2. off
3. for
4. almost
5. also
6. can't
7. cannot
8. about
9. always
10. today
11. until
12. again

1. n o____ w____ **(1 point)**

2. o f____ f____ **(1)**

3. f o____ r **(1)**

4. a____ l____ most **(1)**

5. a____ l____ so **(1)**

6. can '____ t____ **(1)**

7. ca n____ n____ ot **(1)**

8. ab o____ u____ t **(1)**

9. a____ l____ ways **(1)**

10. t____ o____ day **(1)**

11. unt i____ l____ **(1)**

12. ag a____ i____ n **(1)**

Study List On another sheet of paper, write each Spelling Word. Check the list to be sure you spell each word correctly. Order of words may vary. **(2)**

Name _____

Spelling Spree

**Word Switch For each sentence, write a Spelling
Word to take the place of the underlined word or
words.**

1. Let's go ride the roller coaster <u>another time</u>!
2. I'm in a real hurry, so I can't talk <u>at this time</u>.
3. Sofia <u>every time</u> has a box of raisins in her lunch.
4. My mom said that you can come to the beach <u>too</u>, if
   you want.
5. It's been <u>not quite</u> three years since we had a
   snowstorm.
6. They said on the radio that <u>the current day</u> is the
   first day of fall.

1. <u>again **(1 point)**</u>

2. <u>now **(1)**</u>

3. <u>always **(1)**</u>

4. <u>also **(1)**</u>

5. <u>almost **(1)**</u>

6. <u>today **(1)**</u>

**Letter Math Add and subtract letters from the words
below to make Spelling Words. Write the new words.**

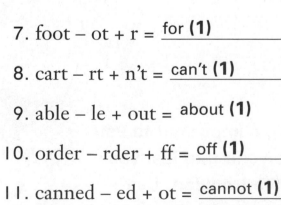

7. foot – ot + r = <u>for **(1)**</u>

8. cart – rt + n't = <u>can't **(1)**</u>

9. able – le + out = <u>about **(1)**</u>

10. order – rder + ff = <u>off **(1)**</u>

11. canned – ed + ot = <u>cannot **(1)**</u>

12. unit – it + til = <u>until **(1)**</u>

Assessment Tip: Total **12** Points

Name _____

Proofreading and Writing

Proofreading Find and circle the four misspelled Spelling Words in this poster. Then write each word correctly.

Spelling Words

1. now
2. off
3. for
4. almost
5. also
6. can't
7. cannot
8. about
9. always
10. today
11. until
12. again

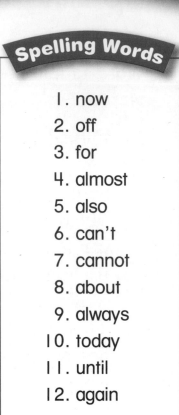

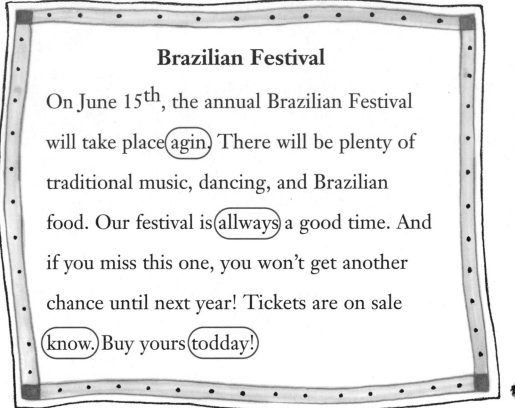

Brazilian Festival

On June 15th, the annual Brazilian Festival will take place (agin). There will be plenty of traditional music, dancing, and Brazilian food. Our festival is (allways) a good time. And if you miss this one, you won't get another chance until next year! Tickets are on sale (know.) Buy yours (todday!)

1. again **(2 points)**

2. always **(2)**

3. now **(2)**

4. today **(2)**

Write a Poem Think about a tradition that's important to you. It can be one shared by a lot of people, or one that just your family shares. Then write a poem about the tradition. Use Spelling Words from the list. Responses will vary. **(2)**

Assessment Tip: Total **10** Points

Name _____

Musical Words

Label each sentence True or False. If the sentence is false, rewrite it to make it correct.

1. A **conga** is played like a trumpet.

   False. A conga is played with the hands. **(2 points)**

   _____

2. **Percussion** instruments are played by being struck or shaken.

   True **(2)**

   _____

3. **Performing** is done with no one around.

   False. Performing is done in front of an audience. **(2)**

   _____

4. A **record** is shaped like a square.

   False. A record is shaped like a circle. **(2)**

   _____

5. **Salsa** is a style of Latin American dance music.

   True **(2)**

   _____

6. A **theater** is a building where plays, movies, or concerts are presented.

   True **(2)**

   _____

Name _____

Categories Chart

Answers will vary.

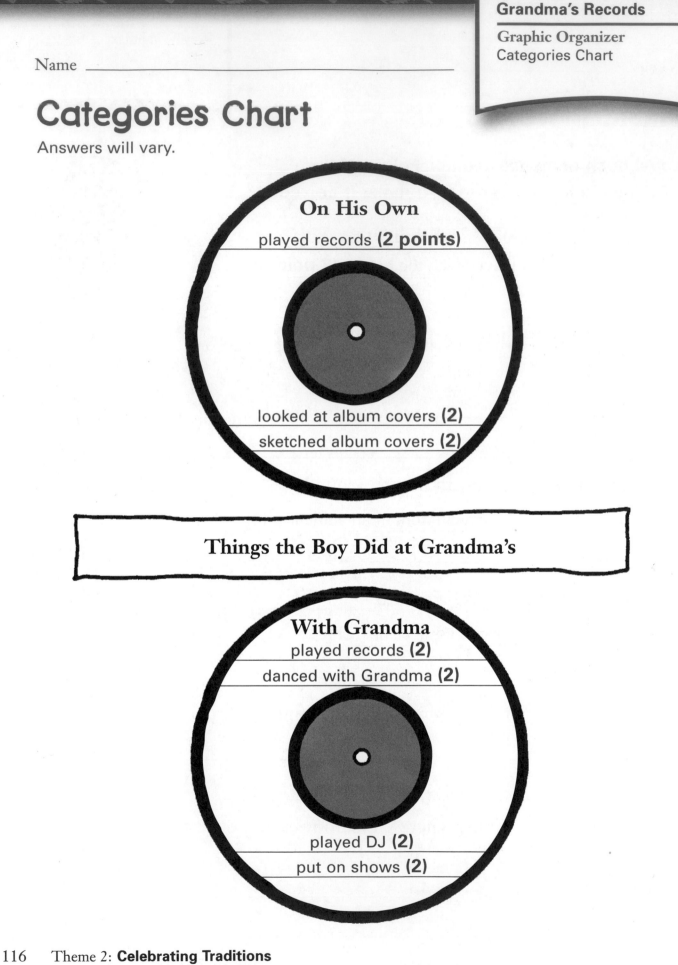

On His Own

played records **(2 points)**

looked at album covers **(2)**

sketched album covers **(2)**

Things the Boy Did at Grandma's

With Grandma

played records **(2)**

danced with Grandma **(2)**

played DJ **(2)**

put on shows **(2)**

116   Theme 2: **Celebrating Traditions**
Assessment Tip: Total **14** Points

Name _____

Read All About It!

Answer the reporter's questions as if you were the grown-up narrator. Use complete sentences.

Answers may vary slightly. Examples are given.

1. Where did you spend your summers as a boy?

   I spent them at my Grandma's apartment in El Barrio,

   New York City. **(2 points)**

2. What did you and your grandmother do all summer?

   We listened to Grandma's records and danced. **(2)**

3. What else did you like to do?

   I liked to draw in my sketchbook. **(2)**

4. Did you ever go anywhere special with Grandma?

   Yes, we once went to see a concert in the Bronx. **(2)**

5. What happened at the concert?

   The lead singer of the band dedicated a song to Grandma. **(2)**

6. What do you do now that you're grown up?

   I'm an artist. **(2)**

Family Categories

Read the story. Then complete the chart on the next page.

No Time to Spare

It's hard to find a good time to get in touch with my Aunt Mickey Sobol. It's even harder to reach my cousins Karen and Ike. That's because they're always busy.

Their day starts at sunup when Karen and Ike head for the barn to feed their sheep. Meanwhile, Aunt Mickey does chores and fixes the lunches. After breakfast, my cousins take the bus to school, and Aunt Mickey leaves for work.

Each day, Aunt Mickey walks a mile to the little store she runs by the lake. People from nearby vacation homes often stop there, so she's always busy.

After school, Karen and Ike head for the animal shelter down the road. Both of them want to be animal doctors, so they like to help with the animals.

After dinner and homework, the family relaxes. Ike usually reads, and Karen talks to a friend on the computer. Aunt Mickey enjoys weaving colorful blankets made of wool from their sheep.

Name _____

Family Categories

Write story details to complete this chart.
Answers may vary.

Family Members

Aunt Mickey Sobol **(1 point)**

Karen **(1)**

Ike **(1)**

Places Near Their Home
their barn

the store near the lake **(1)**

the vacation homes **(1)**

the animal shelter **(1)**

The Sobol Family

Activities
going to school

doing chores **(1)**

running the store **(1)**

helping at the animal shelter **(1)**

relaxing by reading, using the

computer, or weaving **(1)**

Name _____

Perfect Plurals

► Add -*s* to form the plural of most nouns.
  hat/hat**s**

► Add -*es* to form the plural of nouns that end in *ch.*
  lunch/lunch**es**

► When a noun ends with a consonant and *y,*
  change the *y* to *i* and add -*es.*
  penn**y**/penn**ies**

Write the plural of the word that matches each clue in the puzzle. Use the Word Bank for help.

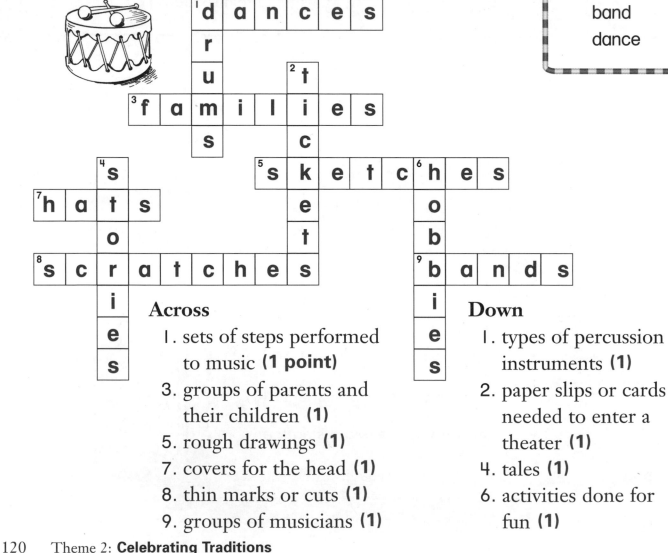

Across

1. sets of steps performed to music **(1 point)**
3. groups of parents and their children **(1)**
5. rough drawings **(1)**
7. covers for the head **(1)**
8. thin marks or cuts **(1)**
9. groups of musicians **(1)**

Down

1. types of percussion instruments **(1)**
2. paper slips or cards needed to enter a theater **(1)**
4. tales **(1)**
6. activities done for fun **(1)**

Assessment Tip: Total **10** Points

Name _____

The Long *o* Sound

To spell a word with the /ō/ sound, remember that this sound can be spelled *oa*, *ow*, or *o*.

/ō/   oa, ow, o   c**oa**ch, bl**ow**, h**o**ld

► In the words *sew* and *though*, the /ō/ sound is spelled *ew* and *ough*.

Write each Spelling Word under its spelling of the /ō/ sound. Order of answers for each category may vary.

Spelling Words

1. coach
2. blow
3. float
4. hold
5. sew
6. though*
7. sold
8. soap
9. row
10. own
11. both
12. most

oa Spelling

coach **(1 point)**

float **(1)**

soap **(1)**

ow Spelling

blow **(1)**

row **(1)**

own **(1)**

o Spelling

hold **(1)**

sold **(1)**

both **(1)**

most **(1)**

Another Spelling

sew **(1)**

though **(1)**

Name _____

Spelling Spree

Word Maze Begin at the arrow and follow the Word Maze to find seven Spelling Words. Write the words in order.

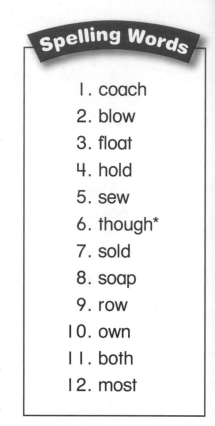

1. coach
2. blow
3. float
4. hold
5. sew
6. though*
7. sold
8. soap
9. row
10. own
11. both
12. most

1. blow **(1 point)**

2. though **(1)**

3. float **(1)**

4. hold **(1)**

5. row **(1)**

6. both **(1)**

7. sold **(1)**

Classifying Write the Spelling Word that belongs in each group of words.

8. have, possess, own **(1)**

9. mend, stitch, sew **(1)**

10. teacher, trainer, coach **(1)**

11. toothpaste, shampoo, soap **(1)**

12. lots, many, most **(1)**

122   Theme 2: **Celebrating Traditions**

Assessment Tip: Total **12** Points

Name _____

Proofreading and Writing

Proofreading Circle the five misspelled Spelling
Words in this poster. Then write each word correctly.

1. coach
2. blow
3. float
4. hold
5. sew
6. though*
7. sold
8. soap
9. row
10. own
11. both
12. most

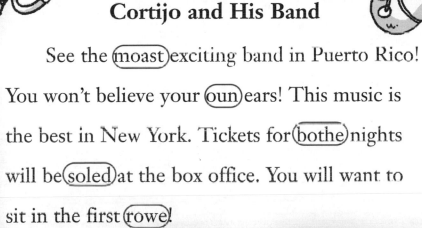

May 19 & 20, Bronx Theatre
Cortijo and His Band

See the (moast) exciting band in Puerto Rico!
You won't believe your (oun) ears! This music is
the best in New York. Tickets for (bothe) nights
will be (soled) at the box office. You will want to
sit in the first (rowe!)

1. most **(2 points)** _____   4. sold **(2)** _____

2. own **(2)** _____   5. row **(2)** _____

3. both **(2)** _____

Write a Story About Yourself Have you ever shared a special
event with a family member or a friend? Maybe it was a concert,
a party, or even a trip.

**On a separate sheet of paper, write about a time when you
shared a special event with a family member or a friend. Tell
what the experience was like. Use Spelling Words from the list.**

Name _____

Word Sort

Parts of a Dictionary Read each word. Then alphabetize the words and place each word with the correct guide words.

snore	lentil	outing
outfit	outgoing	lent
lesson	snowdrift	outlet
snow	leopard	snout

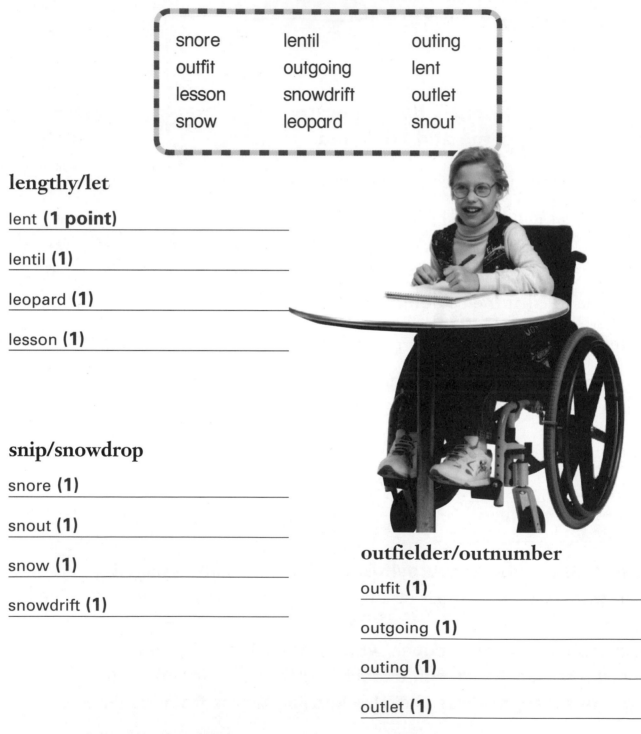

lengthy/let

lent **(1 point)**

lentil **(1)**

leopard **(1)**

lesson **(1)**

snip/snowdrop

snore **(1)**

snout **(1)**

snow **(1)**

snowdrift **(1)**

outfielder/outnumber

outfit **(1)**

outgoing **(1)**

outing **(1)**

outlet **(1)**

124   Theme 2: **Celebrating Traditions**
Assessment Tip: Total **12** Points

Name _____

Capital Letters

Capitalize each proper noun on the list below.

1. carmen maldonado _Carmen Maldonado **(1 point)**_

2. pennsylvania _Pennsylvania **(1)**_

3. tuesday _Tuesday **(1)**_

4. fifth avenue _Fifth Avenue **(1)**_

5. jon carlson smith _John Carlson Smith **(1)**_

6. fourth of july _Fourth of July **(1)**_

7. united states of america _United States of America **(1)**_

8. *the keeping quilt* _The Keeping Quilt **(1)**_

9. mary ellen _Mary Ellen **(1)**_

10. mexico city, mexico _Mexico City, Mexico **(1)**_

Write the proper noun or nouns in each sentence.

11. After school, Dad took me to the library. _Dad **(1)**_

12. We will go to the Westfield Fair on Saturday _Westfield Fair, Saturday **(1)**_

13. Liz wants to visit Colorado. _Liz, Colorado **(1)**_

14. My family plans to travel in Canada. _Canada **(1)**_

15. We will go during the last week of June. _June **(1)**_

Name _____

Charting Capital Letters

This chart shows common and proper nouns. Add one more proper noun for each common noun in the chart.

Answers will vary. Suggested answers are given.

	Common Noun	Proper Noun
people	author	Eric Velasquez _Maurice Sendak_ **(1 point)**
	family member	Grandma _Uncle Jim_ **(1)**
places	country	Spain _Mexico_ **(1)**
	state	Ohio _Illinois_ **(1)**
	city	Detroit _Philadelphia_ **(1)**
	street	Elm Street _Allen Road_ **(1)**
	school	Vale Elementary School _Public School 41_ **(1)**
	store	Blue Goose Pet Shop _The Music Shop_ **(1)**
things	river	Rio Grande _Ohio River_ **(1)**
	month	September _February_ **(1)**
	day	Wednesday _Thursday_ **(1)**
	language	Spanish _French_ **(1)**

Assessment Tip: Total **12** Points

Name _____

Proper Nouns

Remember that titles and their abbreviations, when used with a person's name, begin with a capital letter. Use a capital letter for a person's initials. End abbreviated titles with a period.

Proofread the letter below. Find the proper nouns and titles that need capital letters. Look for abbreviations that need periods. Use the proofreading marks to show the correction. (**1 point** for each correction.)

Proofreading Marks	
Make a small letter:	Çity
Make a capital letter:	boston
Add a period:	Mr⊙

Mr. Jason Brown

326 winter Drive

Brooklyn, NY 11236

Dear Jason,

Hello from puerto rico! My family and I are staying in santurce with our friend dr. R. T. vasquez. My grandmother, Carmen, grew up here.

Later we will visit san juan, which is a big city. On our way back to New york, we will stop in miami, florida.

I can't wait to show my pictures to you and sam. Our teacher, ms. miller, will love the photographs of gardens.

See you soon,

eric

Name _____

A Character Sketch

Use this page to help you plan a character sketch. Write whom your character sketch will be about. Then write at least two interesting details about what the person looks like, what the person says and does, and how you feel about the person. The details should help you to describe the person.

Answers will vary.

My Character

_____

_____

How the Person Looks

1. **(2 points)** _____

2. _____

3. _____

What the Person Does

1. **(2)** _____

2. _____

3. _____

What the Person Says

1. **(2)** _____

_____

2. _____

_____

3. _____

_____

My Feelings About the Person

1. **(2)** _____

2. _____

3. _____

Write your character sketch on a separate sheet of paper.
Use the details above. (2)

Assessment Tip: Total **10** Points

Name _____

Correcting Run-On Sentences

▶ Two or more sentences that run together
  make a **run-on sentence**.

▶ Correct run-on sentences by making separate sentences.
  Add sentence end marks and capital letters where they are needed.

Run-On Sentence:

My friend Patricia loves to dance, she studies ballet every Saturday.

Corrected Sentences:

My friend Patricia loves to dance. She studies ballet every Saturday.

If the sentence is correct, write Correct. **If it is a run-on sentence,
write it as two sentences.**

1. My favorite singer is Gloria Estefan, she sings great songs.

   My favorite singer is Gloria Estefan. She sings great songs. **(2 points)**

   _____

2. My father runs a restaurant in town, he's the best cook in the world.

   My father runs a restaurant in town. He's the best cook in the world. **(2)**

   _____

3. My mother is a math teacher at Yorkstone High School.

   Correct **(2)**

   _____

4. My sister Tasha loves gymnastics, she does the best cartwheels.

   My sister Tasha loves gymnastics. She does the best cartwheels. **(2)**

   _____

Name _____

Word Search

Write the letter of the correct definition next to each word. Then find the words in the puzzle and circle them.

1. wealth c **(1)**

2. royalty b **(1)**

3. collection e **(1)**

4. embroidered a **(1)**

5. symbols d **(1)**

6. flourish f **(1)**

a. decorated by sewing
b. kings and queens
c. lots of money or belongings
d. drawings that stand for something
e. a group of items with something in common
f. a showy waving motion

E	M	B	R	O	I	D	E	R	E	D	D	D
K	J	J	M	F	C	O	Q	W	H	R	G	N
O	L	U	J	Y	R	R	O	Y	A	L	T	Y
R	O	Q	I	P	C	C	O	S	H	T	C	A
X	S	L	D	E	E	O	W	V	E	O	J	N
F	P	X	C	C	O	L	L	E	C	T	O	R
H	L	J	J	M	F	L	O	U	R	I	S	H
L	V	I	M	G	C	E	U	U	N	N	J	B
N	E	F	W	I	M	C	P	W	W	D	J	S
S	S	W	E	A	L	T	H	L	P	Z	K	J
S	E	C	J	W	S	I	J	E	L	M	E	L
W	Y	S	Y	M	B	O	L	S	U	R	Q	W
N	T	R	J	B	V	N	D	Y	Y	S	X	O

Assessment Tip: Total **6** Points

Name _____

Cluster Maps

Answers may vary. Students may find more than four details about each topic given. Possible answers shown here; accept reasonable responses.

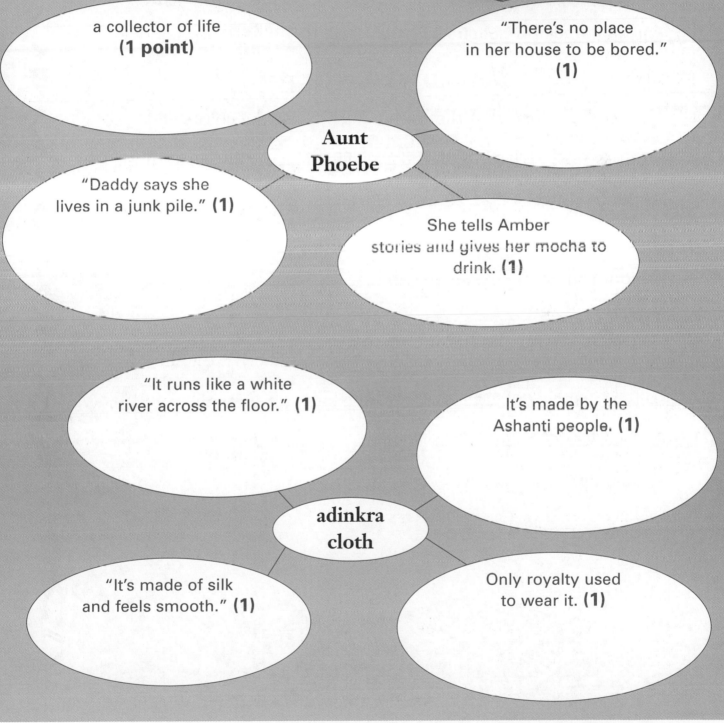

a collector of life
(1 point)

"There's no place
in her house to be bored."
(1)

**Aunt
Phoebe**

"Daddy says she
lives in a junk pile." **(1)**

She tells Amber
stories and gives her mocha to
drink. **(1)**

"It runs like a white
river across the floor." **(1)**

It's made by the
Ashanti people. **(1)**

**adinkra
cloth**

"It's made of silk
and feels smooth." **(1)**

Only royalty used
to wear it. **(1)**

Name _____

What the Cloth Says

Complete these sentences about *The Talking Cloth*.
Answers will vary.

Aunt Phoebe tells Amber about many things. Today they

talk about <u>adinkra cloth from Ghana/Africa. **(2 points)**</u>. At one

time, only <u>royalty **(1)**</u> wore it.

Amber learns that the cloth talks because the colors and

symbols <u>send a message/mean something **(2)**</u>. If the cloth is

white, that means <u>joy **(1)**</u>. If it is blue,

that means <u>love **(1)**</u>. The symbols on it

stand for ideas like <u>faith/power **(1)**</u> and

<u>love **(1)**</u>.

Aunt Phoebe wraps the cloth around Amber. Now she

feels as if she's an <u>Ashanti princess **(1)**</u> with

<u>people who've also worn the cloth **(2)**</u> gathered

around her.

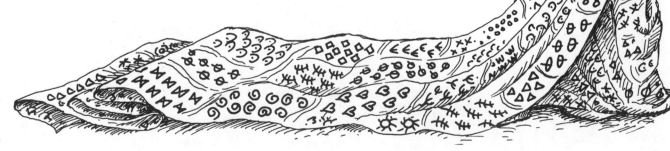

Assessment Tip: Total **12** Points

Name _____

Details for Playing

Read the story. Then complete the chart on the next page.

Not for Sale

As Zack walked along, he passed stores with window displays that didn't interest him. Then he came to a store window full of old, worn things. A strange object caught his eye. The wood was dark and shiny smooth. It was long, about as long as Zack's arm, and had six little bowls along each of its sides. At each end was a larger bowl, which made fourteen little bowls in all.

Curious, Zack went inside for a better look. Noting Zack's interest, the shopkeeper explained that the wooden object was a game board carved by an Ashanti artist in Ghana, Africa. The shopkeeper pulled up two chairs and told Zack to sit down. Then he scooped out some brown seeds from one of the bowls and showed Zack how to play *wari*, an Ashanti board game.

At least once a week Zack stopped by the shop to play *wari* with Mr. Oban, the shopkeeper. Both he and Mr. Oban enjoyed playing. And when they finished, Mr. Oban always put the game board away in the back room. It was no longer for sale.

Theme 2: **Celebrating Traditions**   133

Name _____

Details for Playing

continued

**Complete this chart. List details from
the story "Not for Sale."** Answers may vary.

List of Details
the game board
1. It's made of dark, shiny wood with fourteen little bowls carved into it. **(1)**
2. It was carved by an Ashanti artist. **(1)**
3. It's used for a game called *wari*. **(1)**
4. It's no longer for sale. **(1)**
Zack's feelings
1. He's curious about the wooden object. **(1)**
2. He enjoys playing *wari*. **(1)**
Zack's actions
1. He notices the wooden object in the window. **(1)**
2. He goes inside for a better look. **(1)**
3. He learns how to play *wari*. **(1)**
4. He and Mr. Oban play the game often. **(1)**

Assessment Tip: Total **10** Points

Name _____

Shorten It!

A **contraction** is the short way of saying or writing two words.
The apostrophe (') takes the place of one or more letters.
Fill in the spaces below to show how contractions are formed.

1. he   +   is   =   he's **(1 point)**

2. she   +   will   =   she'll **(1)**

3. was   +   not   =   wasn't **(1)**

4. they   +   are   =   they're **(1)**

5. I   +   will   =   I'll **(1)**

6. it **(1)** _____   +   is **(1)** _____   =   it's

7. you **(1)** _____   +   are **(1)** _____   =   you're

8. has **(1)** _____   +   not **(1)** _____   =   hasn't

9. is **(1)** _____   +   not **(1)** _____   =   isn't

10. we **(1)** _____   +   are **(1)** _____   =   we're

Name _____

Three-Letter Clusters

When two or more consonants with different sounds are written together, they form a **consonant cluster**. When you are spelling a word that has a consonant cluster, say the word aloud and listen for the different consonant sounds. Remember, some words begin with the consonant clusters *spr*, *str*, and *thr*.

spring   **str**ong   **thr**ow

Some other words have unexpected spelling patterns.

► A beginning /n/ sound may be spelled *kn*, as in **kn**ee. (The *k* is silent.)

► A beginning /r/ sound may be spelled *wr*, as in **wr**ap. (The *w* is silent.)

► A final /ch/ sound may be spelled *tch*, as in pa**tch**. (The *t* is silent.)

Spelling Words

1. spring
2. knee
3. throw
4. patch
5. strong
6. wrap
7. three
8. watch
9. street
10. know
11. spread
12. write

Write each Spelling Word under its proper category.
Order of answers for each category may vary.

Three-Letter Clusters

spring **(1 point)** _____

throw **(1)** _____

strong **(1)** _____

three **(1)** _____

street **(1)** _____

spread **(1)** _____

Unexpected Consonant Patterns

knee **(1)** _____

patch **(1)** _____

wrap **(1)** _____

watch **(1)** _____

know **(1)** _____

write **(1)** _____

Assessment Tip: Total **12** Points

Name _____

Spelling Spree

Hink Pinks Write the Spelling Word that fits the clue and rhymes with the given word.

Example: just-born twins **new** _____ *two*

1. a ball tossed to a baby   **low** _____

2. jam or jelly   **bread** _____

3. cord for a kite on a day in May   _____ **string**

4. you and two friends on a school holiday   _____ **free**

5. a tidy block to live on   **neat** _____

6. plastic covering on a bottle top   **cap** _____

1. throw **(1 point)**   4. three **(1)**

2. spread **(1)**   5. street **(1)**

3. spring **(1)**   6. wrap **(1)**

Finding Words Write the Spelling Words in each of these words.

7. patchwork   patch **(1)**

8. headstrong   strong **(1)**

9. kneecap   knee **(1)**

10. wristwatch   watch **(1)**

11. knowing   know **(1)**

12. writer   write **(1)**

Theme 2: **Celebrating Traditions**   137
Assessment Tip: Total **12** Points

Name _____

Proofreading and Writing

Proofreading Circle the five misspelled Spelling Words in this character sketch. Then write each word correctly on the lines below.

1. spring
2. knee
3. throw
4. patch
5. strong
6. wrap
7. three
8. watch
9. street
10. know
11. spread
12. write

Amber's aunt has been everywhere. Aunt Phoebe takes a long trip to a faraway place every (springe). She has been to Africa (thee) times. When she visits a foreign country, she wants to (nowe) what it is like to live there. Every time she walks down a new street, she likes to (wache) the people carefully. She notices how they dress and listens to how they speak. Later, she always takes the time to (rite) to Amber about her experiences. I admire Aunt Phoebe because she is always learning something new.

1. spring **(2 points)**

2. three **(2)**

3. know **(2)**

4. watch **(2)**

5. write **(2)**

Write a Thank-You Note Has a relative or friend ever given you a special or unusual gift? What was it that made it special?

On a separate sheet of paper, write a thank-you note for the gift. Make sure to tell the person you are thanking why the gift is special to you. Use Spelling Words from the list. Responses will vary. **(2)**

Assessment Tip: Total **12** Points

Name _____

Rhyming Crossword

Complete the crossword puzzle by writing the correct rhyme for each word. Remember that a rhyming word has the same end sound as another word. Choose your answers from the words in the box.

Vocabulary

trip
map
lace
cause
wealth
silk
smiles
sled
smells
might

Across

2. Object used to go across snow. Rhymes with *said*. **(1 point)**
3. A happy person does this. Rhymes with *miles*. **(1)**
7. A piece of string used to tie a shoe. Rhymes with *face*. **(1)**
8. Riches. Rhymes with *health*. **(1)**
9. A voyage. Rhymes with *lip*. **(1)**
10. Drawings of the earth's surface. Rhymes with *traps*. **(1)**

Down

1. What your nose does. Rhymes with *tells*. **(1)**
4. Strength. Rhymes with *right*. **(1)**
5. A smooth, shiny fabric. Rhymes with *milk*. **(1)**
6. A reason. Rhymes with *pause*. **(1)**

Name _____

Circling Nouns

**Circle each singular common noun in the sentences below.
Underline each plural common noun.**

1. Aunt Phoebe collects many <u>things</u>. **(1 point)**

2. The (cloth) is embroidered in <u>section</u>. **(1)**

3. The (fabric) has no <u>patches</u>. **(1)**

4. The <u>patterns</u> show many <u>colors</u> and <u>shapes</u>. **(1)**

5. Phoebe gave her (niece) two <u>boxes</u>. **(1)**

6. Inside, she found two colorful <u>dresses</u>. **(1)**

Write each plural noun in the correct column below.

Add -*s* to form the plural	Add -*es* to form the plural
things **(1 point)**	patches **(1)**
sections **(1)**	boxes **(1)**
patterns **(1)**	dresses **(1)**
colors **(1)**	
shapes **(1)**	

Name _____

Puzzling Plurals

Complete the puzzle by writing the plural of each noun.
Each noun is used only once. Some letters are filled in
to help you get started. (2 points for each answer)

Across

princess _princesses_

basket _baskets_

number _numbers_

thing _things_

tale _tales_

Down

symbol _symbols_

box _boxes_

word _words_

pattern _patterns_

dress _dresses_

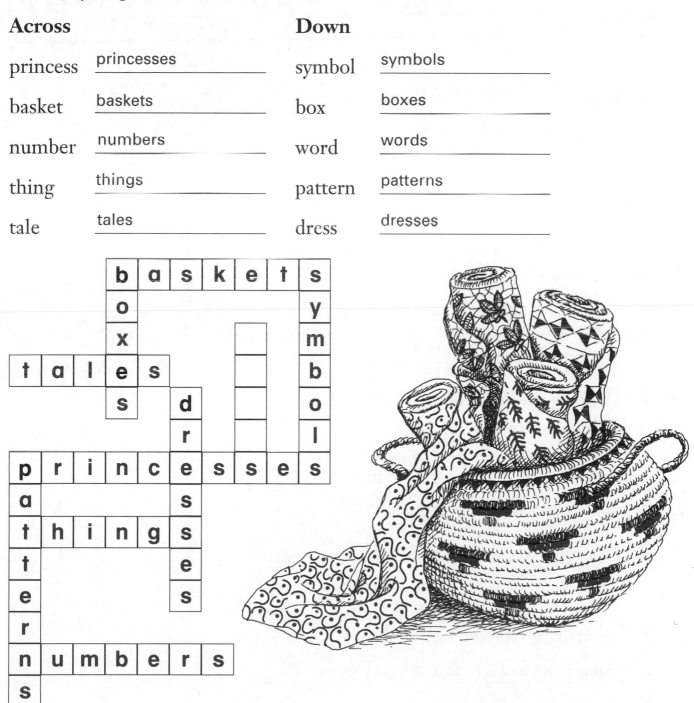

Name _____

Using Exact Nouns

Write a noun that is more exact than each general noun below. Answers will vary. Possible answers given.

1. animal   wolf **(1 point)**

2. tree   elm **(1)**

3. food   apple pie **(1)**

4. container   basket **(1**

5. group   family **(1)**

Read each sentence below. Then rewrite the sentence on the line, substituting an exact noun for the general noun or word in parentheses.

6. Amber visited her favorite (person).

   Amber visited her favorite aunt. **(1)**

7. They shared a hot (drink) together.

   They shared a hot mocha together. **(1)**

8. Phoebe showed Amber a (thing).

   Phoebe showed Amber a cloth. **(1)**

9. The (thing) was covered with many (shapes).

   The cloth was covered with many symbols. **(1)**

10. One (shape) looked like a spinning (circle).

   One symbol looked like a spinning wheel. **(1)**

Name _____

Writing an Answer to a Question

When you write an answer to a question, follow these guidelines.

► Read the question carefully.

► Look for key words to help you decide what information the question is asking for.

► Give facts and examples that provide the information asked for.

For each question, write your answer on the lines. Write the start of the answer on the first answer line. Write the rest of the answer on the other answer lines. Answers will vary.

1. **Question:** What holiday do you enjoy most? Explain why.
   Turn the question into a statement. (2 points)

   _____

   Give facts that answer the question.

   (2) _____

   _____

2. **Question:** What place would you like to visit most? Explain why.
   Turn the question into a statement.

   (2) _____

   Give facts that answer the question.

   (2) _____

   _____

Name _____

Writing Complete Sentences

A complete sentence contains both a naming part
and an action part.

Naming Part	**Action Part**
Aunt Phoebe	bought the adinkra cloth in Africa.

A sentence fragment is an incomplete sentence that has
just one sentence part.

Fragment (naming part only) The Ashanti people.
Fragment (action part only) Made adinkra cloths.

A complete sentence begins with a capital letter and ends
with the correct end punctuation.z

Read each item. Write *Complete Sentence* **if the sentence
has both a naming part and an action part. If the item is a
sentence fragment, make it a complete sentence by adding
words. Write your complete sentence correctly.**

1. Means gold or riches. Possible answer: A yellow cloth means

   gold or riches. **(2 points)**

2. Amber and her father. Possible answer: Amber and her father visit

   Aunt Phoebe. **(2)**

3. Aunt Phoebe tells stories to Amber. Complete Sentence **(2)**

4. Drinks hot mocha. Possible answer: The young girl drinks hot mocha. **(2)**

Assessment Tip: Total **8** Points

Name _____

What Do You Think?

Answer the questions below. Use your glossary if you need help. Answers will vary.

1. Who are some of your ancestors? Where did they live?

   (2 points) _____

   _____

2. What could someone do to honor his or her

   parents or family members?

   (2) _____

   _____

3. What is something you have learned by imitating another

   person?

   (2) _____

   _____

4. What can you do to show respect for your teacher?

   (2) _____

   _____

5. How should young people act toward their elders?

   (2) _____

   _____

Name _____

Cluster Diagram

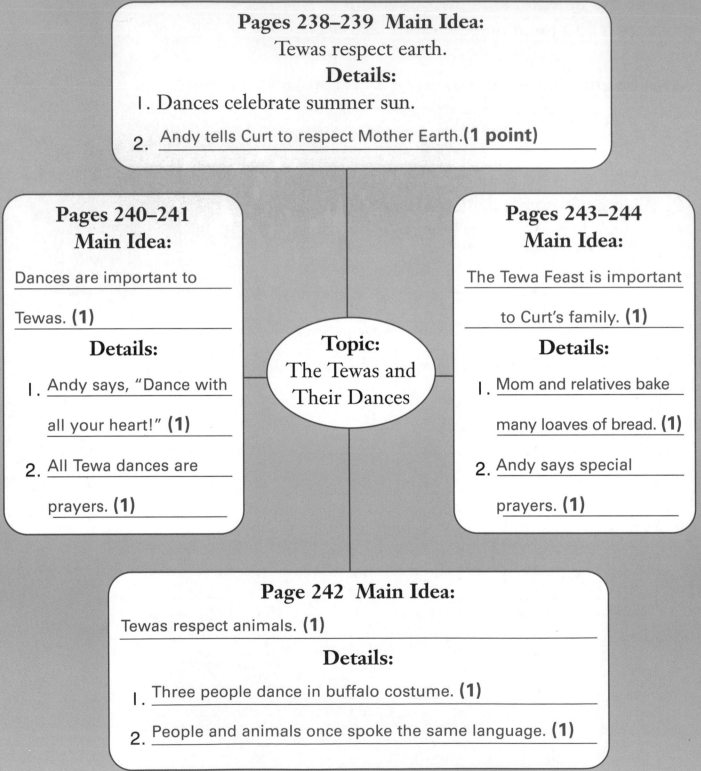

Pages 238–239 Main Idea:
Tewas respect earth.
Details:
1. Dances celebrate summer sun.
2. Andy tells Curt to respect Mother Earth. **(1 point)**

**Pages 240–241
Main Idea:**
Dances are important to

Tewas. **(1)**
Details:
1. Andy says, "Dance with

all your heart!" **(1)**
2. All Tewa dances are

prayers. **(1)**

Topic:
The Tewas and
Their Dances

**Pages 243–244
Main Idea:**
The Tewa Feast is important

to Curt's family. **(1)**
Details:
1. Mom and relatives bake

many loaves of bread. **(1)**
2. Andy says special

prayers. **(1)**

Page 242 Main Idea:
Tewas respect animals. **(1)**
Details:
1. Three people dance in buffalo costume. **(1)**
2. People and animals once spoke the same language. **(1)**

Assessment Tip: Total **10** Points

Name _____

Feast Day Questions

Answer each question about *Dancing Rainbows*.
Use complete sentences. Answers may vary somewhat.
Examples are given.

1. What is Feast Day?

   It is the day the Tewas in San Juan Pueblo, New Mexico, hold a big party to

   honor their patron saint and celebrate the power of the summer sun. **(2 points)**

   _____

2. Why do Curt, Andy, and the other Tewa people dance on Feast Day?

   They dance prayers to cure the sick, give thanks, bring the tribe together,

   ask for good crops, have fun, and bring rain. **(2)**

3. What sounds might you hear on Feast Day in the plaza?

   You might hear the sound of drums and bells, the shuffling of the dancers'

   feet, and singing in Tewa. **(2)**

4. When the Tewas dance, what might you see?

   Dancers of all ages dance many dances, including the Buffalo, Eagle, and

   Comanche Dances. They paint their faces and wear colorful costumes and

   headdresses. **(2)**

5. What did Andy do for his grandson and other young Tewas?

   He started a Tewa dance group for them where they learn traditional

   dances so they can dance at fairs, powwows, and other shows. **(2)**

Assessment Tip: Total **10** Points

Name _____

Mainly Ideas

Read the article. Then complete the diagram on the next page.

All About Eagles

How many different kinds of eagles do you think live in the world? If you guessed about sixty, you'd be right. Some kinds of eagles are large and some are small. Most are strong for their size. Some are even strong enough to lift food weighing almost as much as they do!

Eagles have been used as symbols of power and freedom. Some people call them the "king of birds" because of their strength and brave, proud looks. In 1782, the United States of America chose the bald eagle as its national bird.

Bald eagles are among the larger eagles. They can weigh anywhere from eight to thirteen pounds. These great birds can have wings that spread as much as seven feet across! Their heads are covered with white feathers, making them look "bald" from a distance.

Name _____

Mainly Ideas continued

Complete the diagram with facts from "All About Eagles."

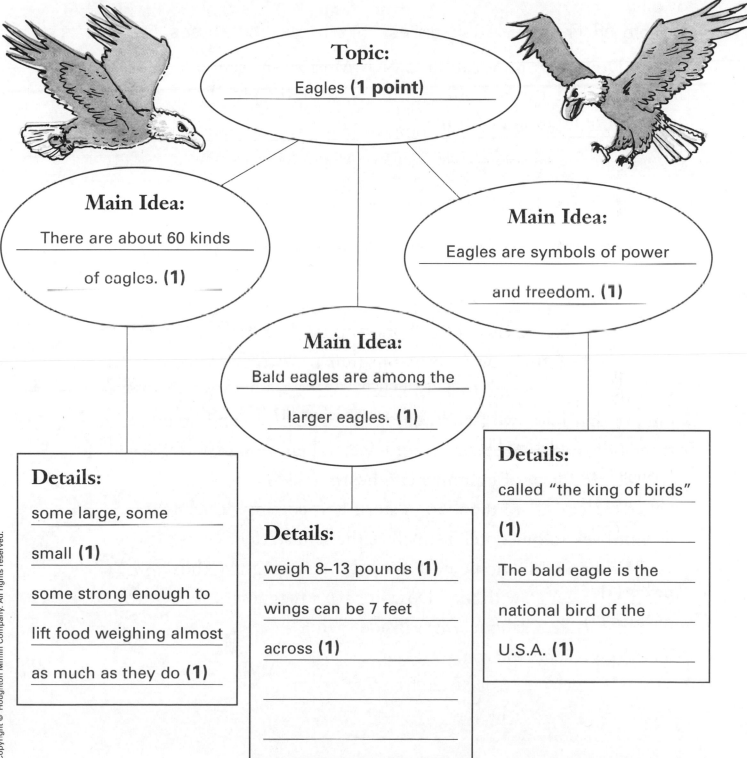

Topic:

Eagles **(1 point)**

Main Idea:

There are about 60 kinds

of eagles. **(1)**

Main Idea:

Eagles are symbols of power

and freedom. **(1)**

Main Idea:

Bald eagles are among the

larger eagles. **(1)**

Details:

some large, some

small **(1)**

some strong enough to

lift food weighing almost

as much as they do **(1)**

Details:

weigh 8–13 pounds **(1)**

wings can be 7 feet

across **(1)**

_____

_____

Details:

called "the king of birds"

(1)

The bald eagle is the

national bird of the

U.S.A. **(1)**

Dancing Rainbows

Structural Analysis
Plurals of Words Ending in
ch, *sh*, *x*, *s*

Name _____

More and More Plurals

Add *-es* to form the plural of a singular noun that ends in *ch*, *sh*, *x*, or *s*.

branch/branch**es**   dish/dish**es**   mix/mix**es**   bus/bus**es**

When Dora went on vacation to New Mexico, she sent a letter to her best friend. In each blank, write the plural form of the noun in parentheses ( ).

November 4

Dear Sally,

New Mexico is a beautiful place to visit. When I look out my hotel window, I can see (bush) <u>bushes **(1 point)**</u>, trees, and mountains. There are rocky deserts too.

Yesterday, we visited two horse (ranch) <u>ranches **(1)**</u>. After I rode a gray pony, we ate our (lunch) <u>lunches **(1)**</u> while sitting on picnic (bench) <u>benches **(1)**</u>. I was so hungry that I ate two (sandwich) <u>sandwiches **(1)**</u> and drank three (glass) <u>glasses **(1)**</u> of juice! Then we saw (flash) <u>flashes **(1)**</u> of lightning and heard (crash) <u>crashes **(1)**</u> of thunder. A storm was coming! Luckily, we got back to our hotel just before the rain started.

When I come home next week, I'm bringing two (box) <u>boxes **(1)**</u> with me. Do you have any (guess) <u>guesses **(1)**</u> about what's inside them? They're presents for you!

Your friend,
Dora

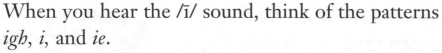

Name _____

The Long *i* Sound

When you hear the /ī/ sound, think of the patterns *igh*, *i*, and *ie*.

/ī/ br**igh**t, w**i**ld, d**ie**

Write each Spelling Word under its spelling of the /ī/ sound. Order of answers for each category may vary.

Spelling Words

1. wild
2. bright
3. die
4. sight
5. child
6. pie
7. fight
8. lie
9. tight
10. tie
11. might
12. mind

igh Spelling

bright **(1 point)** _____

sight **(1)** _____

fight **(1)** _____

tight **(1)** _____

might **(1)** _____

i Spelling

wild **(1)** _____

child **(1)** _____

mind **(1)** _____

ie Spelling

die **(1)** _____

pie **(1)** _____

lie **(1)** _____

tie **(1)** _____

Name _____

Spelling Spree

Sentence Pairs Write the Spelling Word that best completes each pair of sentences.

Example: A jet does not fly low. It flies _high_ .

1. These shoes are not loose. They are _____.
2. My sister is not a grownup. She is a _____.
3. A tiger is not tame. It is _____.
4. I will not have cake for dessert. I will have _____.
5. Neither team won. The score was a _____.
6. The sunshine is not dim today. It is _____.
7. He did not tell the truth. He told a _____.

Spelling Words

1. wild
2. bright
3. die
4. sight
5. child
6. pie
7. fight
8. lie
9. tight
10. tie
11. might
12. mind

1. tight **(1 point)**

2. child **(1)**

3. wild **(1)**

4. pie **(1)**

5. tie **(1)**

6. bright **(1)**

7. lie **(1)**

Missing Letters Each missing letter fits in ABC order between the other two letters. Write the missing letters to spell a Spelling Word.

Example: e _ g   h _ j   m _ o   c _ e   *find*

8. c _ e   h _ j   d _ f

9. l _ n   h _ j   m _ o   c _ e

10. e _ g   h _ j   f _ h   g _ i   s _ u

8. die **(1)**

9. mind **(1)**

10. fight **(1)**

Assessment Tip: Total **10** Points

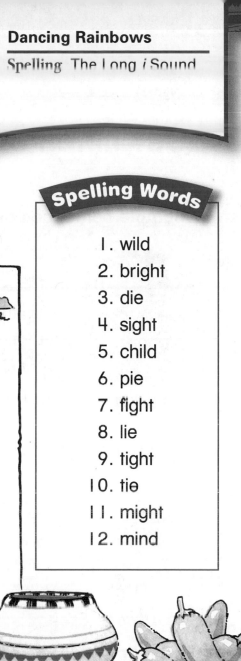

Name _____

Proofreading and Writing

Proofreading Circle the five misspelled Spelling Words in this page from a travel brochure. Then write each word correctly.

Visit Beautiful New Mexico!

Come to New Mexico and discover a land of amazing beauty! Explore wonderful deserts bathed in (brit) sunshine. Hike in our mountains and experience adventure in the (wilde!) Relax your (minde) and body at one of our many resorts. Enjoy the (siet) of colorful hot-air balloons in Albuquerque. Spend a week with us, and you just (mieght) never go home again! That's no lie.

Spelling Words

1. wild
2. bright
3. die
4. sight
5. child
6. pie
7. fight
8. lie
9. tight
10. tie
11. might
12. mind

1. bright **(2 points)**

2. wild **(2)**

3. mind **(2)**

4. sight **(2)**

5. might **(2)**

Write an Explanation The Tewas believe that the eagle is a special animal that carries messages to earth. If you could wear an animal costume, what animal would you choose to be?

On a separate sheet of paper, tell what animal you would choose and explain why you think this animal is special. Use Spelling Words from the list. Responses will vary. **(2)**

Name _____

Definition Derby

Read the dictionary entry for the word *dance*. Then write sample sentences as directed. Answers will vary.

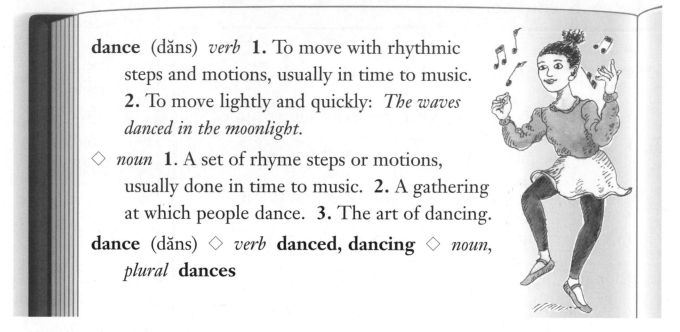

dance (dăns) *verb* **1.** To move with rhythmic steps and motions, usually in time to music. **2.** To move lightly and quickly: *The waves danced in the moonlight.*

◇ *noun* **1.** A set of rhyme steps or motions, usually done in time to music. **2.** A gathering at which people dance. **3.** The art of dancing.

dance (dăns) ◇ *verb* **danced, dancing** ◇ *noun,* *plural* **dances**

1. Write a sentence using the most common meaning of *dance*.

   (2 points)
   _____

2. Write a sentence using noun definition number 3.

   (2)
   _____

3. Write a sentence using noun definition number 1.

   (2)
   _____

4. Write a sentence using verb definition number 2.

   (2)
   _____

5. Write a sentence using the least common meaning of *dance*.

   (2)
   _____

Name _____

Beat the Drum for Plurals

Circle all the plural nouns and write each one in the correctly labeled drum.

1. The Tewa (children) practice dancing.
2. (Men) and (women) prepare for a festival.
3. The (skies) are clear and blue.
4. (Families) arrive from many different (cities).
5. The (parties) are about to begin.
6. (Loaves) of bread are stacked on the table.
7. (People) stomp their (feet).
8. Sweet (candies) are a special treat.

Change *y* to *i* and add *-es*

skies **(2 points)** _____

families **(2)** _____

cities **(2)** _____

parties **(2)** _____

candies **(2)** _____

Special Plural Forms

children **(2)** _____

men **(2)** _____

women **(2)** _____

loaves **(2)** _____

people **(2)** _____

feet **(2)** _____

Name _____

Completing with Plurals

Complete the story by writing the plural form for each noun in parentheses.

1. The <u>skies **(2 points)**</u> are sunny and clear. (sky)

2. All the relatives help bake many <u>loaves **(2)**</u> of bread for the feast. (loaf)

3. Many <u>families **(2)**</u> have come to the celebration. (family)

4. At last, six <u>men **(2)**</u> begin to dance. (man)

5. Their <u>feet **(2)**</u> fly above the ground. (foot)

Assessment Tip: Total **10** Points

Name _____

Proofreading for Noun Endings

Proofread the paragraphs below. Find plurals of nouns that are spelled incorrectly. Circle each misspelled plural. Then write each correctly spelled noun on the lines below. Use a dictionary for help.

After sunrise, the Tewa (mens) and (womens) gather.
Mothers carry their smiling (babys). (Fatheres) walk with
their sons and daughters. People arrive from many (citys).
They look forward to the dances and the (storys).

Three (childs) wear buffalo (costumies). They are
dancers. Their feet move in beautiful (patternes). After the
dance, everyone feasts on (loafs) of bread and tasty treats.

Regular	Ends in consonant + y	Special plurals
fathers **(1 point)**	babies **(1)**	men **(1)**
costumes **(1)**	cities **(1)**	women **(1)**
patterns **(1)**	stories **(1)**	children **(1)**
		loaves **(1)**

Name _____

Writing a News Article

Use this page to plan and organize your news article about a holiday or celebration. When you finish, use the outline to write your article on a separate sheet of paper.

1. Holiday or Celebration _____
   (1 point) _____

2. Who? _____
   (1) _____

3. What? _____
   (1) _____

4. When? _____
   (1) _____

5. Where? _____
   (1) _____

6. Why? _____
   (1) _____

7. How? _____
   (1) _____

8. Interesting Opening Sentence _____
   (2) _____

9. Interesting Headline **(1)** _____

Assessment Tip: Total **10** Points

Name _____

Newspaper Article

Audience A good newspaper article includes details that help the audience picture what they did not witness themselves.

Read the newspaper article. Then answer each question based on some facts or details from the article.

> In the past month, San Juan Pueblo has had no rain. The elders of the Tewa tribe who live there have decided to hold a rain dance. The dancing will begin at nine in the morning and last until noon. The purpose of the dance is to ask the Tewa ancestors to bring rain. Andy Garcia is an elder of the tribe. He says that the Tewa believe that their ancestors come back as raindrops to water their crops and give them water to drink.

1. Who are the Tewa?

   Answers may vary. The Tewa are a tribe of Native Americans. **(2 points)**

2. Where will the rain dance be held?

   Answers may vary. The rain dance will be held at San Juan Pueblo. **(2)**

3. What would make an interesting beginning to the article?

   Answers will vary. **(3)**

   _____

   _____

4. What would make an interesting headline for this article?

   Answers will vary. **(3)**

Congratulations! You are a good reporter! Now write your new, improved article on a separate piece of paper.

Name _____

A Blossoming Crossword

In the crossword, write the vocabulary word that matches each clue. Write one letter in each box.

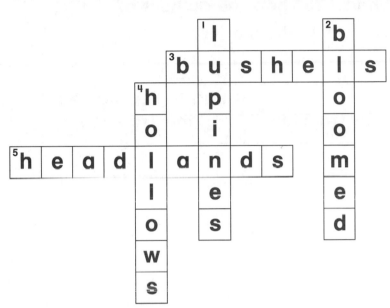

Vocabulary

bloomed
bushels
headlands
hollows
lupines

Across

3. large amounts of something **(2 points)**
5. high lands near the water **(2)**

Down

1. blue and purple flowers **(2)**
2. what the flowers did when they opened **(2)**
4. little valleys **(2)**

Name _____

Celebrating Chinese New Year

Use story details to finish the chart. Tell how the authors of these stories feel about the traditions in the stories.

Answers will vary. Accept reasonable responses.

Story	Details About the Tradition	Author's Feelings About the Tradition
Miss Rumphius Tradition: making the world more beautiful	1. Miss Rumphius's grandfather asked her to make the world more beautiful. **(1)** 2. She plants lupines. **(1)** 3. tells Alice to make the world more beautiful **(1)**	The author feels that making the world more beautiful is important. **(2)**
Celebrating Chinese New Year Tradition: Chinese New Year	1. Families go visiting and bring gifts. **(1)** 2. share a meal **(1)** 3. eat special dishes such as duck **(1)**	The author feels that this tradition helps bring families together. **(2)**

Assessment Tip: Total **10** Points

Traditions Diagram

Fill in the Venn diagram below with details about the traditions in *Miss Rumphius* and *The Keeping Quilt*.

Wording of answers may vary.

Miss Rumphius

Tradition:

making the world a better place
(2 points)

Created by:

Miss Rumphius's grandfather
(1)

How Miss Rumphius does it:

plants lupine seeds
(1)

Places she does it:

1. Sample answers: fields, headlands, highways, **(1)**
2. schoolhouse, church yard
(1)

Passed on to:

little Alice
(1)

Both Traditions:

Sample answer: are passed down over time
(1)

Sample answer: make many people happy
(1)

The Family in *The Keeping Quilt*

Tradition:

family quilt
(2)

Created by: Anna's mother and neighborhood ladies
(1)

Used for: Sample answers: tablecloth, wedding
1. huppa, celebrating birthdays, keeping **(1)**
2. people warm.
(1)

Passed on to:

generations of women
(1)

Assessment Tip: Total **15** Points

Name _____

Words for a Feast

Key Words Read each sentence. Then circle the letter of the word or phrase that has almost the same meaning as the underlined word.

1. The queen decided to bring everyone in the kingdom together. She wanted to celebrate her country's unity.
   A. togetherness   B. beauty   C. happiness
   (2 points)

2. The king and queen would be the hosts of the biggest party in history.
   A. people who visit other people
   B. people who go to fancy hotels
   C. people who invite other people over **(2)**

3. The chef had never cooked for so many people before.
   A. leader   B. cook **(2)**   C. firefighter

4. To feed the whole kingdom, he would have to make a great feast.
   A. fancy meal **(2)**
   B. cooking pot
   C. breakfast cereal

5. He cooked cakes with seven layers and other elaborate dishes.
   A. boring
   B. fancy **(2)**
   C. easy

Assessment Tip: Total **10** Points

Name _____

Test Practice

Use the three steps you've learned to complete these sentences about *Celebrating Chinese New Year*. Fill in the circle next to the best answer.

1. Chinese New Year begins with a _____. **(5 points)**
   - ● visit with relatives
   - ○ big dinner
   - ○ parade
   - ○ trip to the grocery

2. The main idea of *Celebrating Chinese New Year* is that the holiday is a time when _____. **(5)**
   - ● families get together
   - ○ Ryan helps his dad prepare a special meal
   - ○ people do not work
   - ○ people eat too much food

3. Ryan's father probably cooks _____. **(5)**
   - ○ only duck and chicken
   - ○ hamburgers and hot dogs
   - ● tasty holiday meals
   - ○ mostly cakes and pies

4. **Connecting/Comparing** The quilt in *The Keeping Quilt* is like the duck and chicken dish prepared by Ryan's father because both remind people of _____. **(5)**
   - ○ happiness
   - ● family unity
   - ○ national pride
   - ○ a new year

Continue on page 166.
Theme 2: **Celebrating Traditions**   165

Test Practice continued

5. The author of Celebrating *Chinese New Year* wrote this article to _____. **(5 points)**

   ○ explain how to cook a duck

   ● tell about a special Chinese tradition

   ○ describe Ryan's family

   ○ persuade readers to visit relatives more often

6. If Ryan did not visit his aunt during the first three days of the Chinese New Year, she might _____. **(5)**

   ○ send him a special gift   ○ prepare him a meal

   ○ invite him to go on a trip   ● be angry with him

7. Ryan's family shops early for the New Year's Day meal because _____. **(5)**

   ○ it is bad luck to shop on New Year's Day

   ○ Ryan's father works at a restaurant on New Year's Day

   ○ grocery stores sometimes run out of duck and chicken

   ● the New Year's Day feast takes many days to prepare

8. **Connecting/Comparing** Think about Ryan in *Celebrating Chinese New Year* and Curt in *Dancing Rainbows*. When they grow up, they will probably both _____. **(5)**

   ○ go to a parade to celebrate New Year's Day

   ● teach their children their families' traditions

   ○ learn how to perform the buffalo dance

   ○ go to San Francisco for a holiday celebration

A Community of Categories

Read the list of things found in the community where Miss Rumphius lives. Write each item in the correct box.

Word Bank

church	headlands	house	schoolhouse
fields	highways	lanes	seeds
flowers	hills	lupines	stones

Buildings in a Community
church (**1 point**)
house (**1**)
schoolhouse (**1**)

Places in a Community
fields (**1**)
headlands (**1**)
highways (**1**)
hills (**1**)
lanes (**1**)

Things in a Garden
flowers (**1**)
lupines (**1**)
seeds (**1**)
stones (**1**)

What's It All About?

Read the paragraphs. Then answer the questions.

My family comes from Spain. Our New Year's celebration is a bit different from that of other people. To begin with, we invite friends over for dinner. That might not sound strange, but we eat dinner very late. People don't start arriving at our house until 9 or 10 P.M.

By the time dinner is done, it's close to midnight. Then everyone gathers around a large bowl of grapes. For each toll of the bell, you eat one grape. That's twelve total, one for each month of the year. By doing so, you are supposed to have good luck in the coming year.

What is the topic of this paragraph?

the New Year's celebration in one family **(2 point)**

What is the main idea?

The Spanish New Year's celebration includes a late dinner and grapes. **(2)**

What are three supporting details?

People don't begin to arrive for dinner until 9 or 10 P.M. **(2)**

Everyone eats 12 grapes. **(2)**

Following this tradition is supposed to bring good luck. **(2)**

Assessment Tip: Total **10** Points

Name _____

Contraction Math

Write the two words that each contraction stands for as an equation. See the example below.

you're = you + are

1. he'll = he + will **(1 point)** _____

2. isn't = is + not **(1)** _____

3. she's = she + is **(1)** _____

4. they'll = they + will **(1)** _____

5. shouldn't = should + not **(1)** _____

6. we're = we + are **(1)** _____

7. you'll = you + will **(1)** _____

8. don't = do + not **(1)** _____

9. they're = they + are **(1)** _____

10. you're = you + are **(1)** _____

Name _____

Rhyme It!

To complete the poem below, choose a word from the box that rhymes with each underlined word, and write it on the line.

We all went walking one by <u>one</u>,
And then we stopped to have some <u>fun **(1 point)**</u>.

We all went walking two by <u>two</u>,
And then we stopped to eat some <u>stew **(1)**</u>.

We all went walking three by <u>three</u>,
And then we stopped to climb a <u>tree **(1)**</u>.

We all went walking four by <u>four</u>,
And then we stopped at the candy <u>store **(1)**</u>.

We all went walking five by <u>five</u>,
And then we stopped to scuba <u>dive **(1)**</u>.

We all went walking six by <u>six</u>,
And then we stopped to play some <u>tricks **(1)**</u>.

We all went walking seven by <u>seven</u>,
And then we stopped to count to <u>eleven **(1)**</u>.

We all went walking eight by <u>eight</u>,
And then we stopped to roller <u>skate **(1)**</u>.

We all went walking nine by <u>nine</u>,
And then we stopped to read a <u>sign **(1)**</u>.

We all went walking ten by <u>ten</u>,
And then we said, "Let's start <u>again **(1)**</u>!"

Word Bank

skate
stew
again
fun
tricks
eleven
tree
sign
dive
store

Assessment Tip: Total **10** Points

Name _____

Spelling Review

Write Spelling Words from the list to answer the questions. Order of answers in each category may vary.

1–9. Which nine words have the long *a* or long *e* sound?

1. lay **(1 point)**
2. feel **(1)**
3. seem **(1)**
4. three **(1)**
5. speak **(1)**
6. need **(1)**
7. leave **(1)**
8. paint **(1)**
9. street **(1)**

10–16. Which seven words have the long *o* sound?

10. hold **(1)**
11. own **(1)**
12. most **(1)**
13. float **(1)**
14. row **(1)**
15. both **(1)**
16. know **(1)**

17–22. Which six words have the long *i* sound?

17. wild **(1)**
18. might **(1)**
19. lie **(1)**
20. mind **(1)**
21. bright **(1)**
22. tie **(1)**

23–25. Which three words end with these letters?
23. ____tch   24. ____ead   25. ____ap

23. patch **(1)**
24. spread **(1)**
25. wrap **(1)**

Spelling Words

1. lay
2. feel
3. hold
4. wild
5. might
6. paint
7. seem
8. patch
9. three
10. own
11. speak
12. need
13. lie
14. most
15. spread
16. float
17. row
18. leave
19. both
20. wrap
21. know
22. mind
23. street
24. bright
25. tie

Assessment Tip: Total **25** Points

Name _____

Spelling Spree

Rhyme Time Write the Spelling Word that rhymes with
the word in dark print.

Example: A plump kitty is a ____fat____ **cat.**

1. A nice brain is a **kind** _mind **(1 point)**_____.

2. An animal life jacket is a **goat** _float **(1)**_____.

3. An unreal piece of clothing is a _tie **(1)**_____ **lie.**

4. Baby triplets are a **wee** _three **(1)**_____.

Word Search Underline the eight hidden
Spelling Words. Then write the words.

Example: abe<u>needle</u>an ____needle____

5. reda<u>wild</u>ell

6. <u>ymight</u>aledfl

7. enr<u>street</u>alp

8. kn<u>paint</u>ilke

9. teril<u>oneed</u>um

10. gr<u>patch</u>ibror

11. olgera<u>spread</u>

12. wri<u>lleave</u>kn

5. _wild **(1)**_____

6. _might **(1)**_____

7. _street **(1)**_____

8. _paint **(1)**_____

9. _need **(1)**_____

10. _patch **(1)**_____

11. _spread **(1)**_____

12. _leave **(1)**_____

Assessment Tip: Total **12** Points

Spelling Words

1. paint
2. leave
3. might
4. need
5. mind
6. tie
7. spread
8. float
9. three
10. wild
11. patch
12. street

Name _____

Proofreading and Writing

Proofreading Circle the six misspelled Spelling Words in this play. Then write each word correctly.

Grandpa: Let's (rapp) the gifts in (brite) yellow paper.

Joe: We can (laye) it on the table for Mom.

Grandpa: Be careful how you (hoald) it.

Joe: You (kno) we (bouth) did a good job!

1. lay
2. most
3. wrap
4. lie
5. feel
6. seem
7. hold
8. speak
9. own
10. bright
11. row
12. both
13. know
14. mind

1. wrap **(1)**   3. lay **(1)**   5. know **(1)**

2. bright **(1)**   4. hold **(1)**   6. both **(1)**

Complete a Letter Use Spelling Words to complete the following letter.

Thanksgiving makes me 7. feel **(1)** very happy. Our family has its 8. own **(1)** traditions. My grandfather will 9. speak **(1)** his 10. mind **(1)** about sharing with others. A feast will 11. lie **(1)** on the table, with many plates in a 12. row **(1)**. The 13. most **(1)** simple dishes 14. seem **(1)** even tastier then.

Write a Description On a separate sheet of paper, describe a celebration you enjoy. Use the Spelling Words.

Responses will vary. **(2)**

Name _____

Finding Common Nouns

Find the common nouns in the announcement. Write each common noun in the correct garden bed below.

The students at our school will plant a garden. We will use the area behind the gym. All boys and girls can help! A parent will bring seeds and tools. You can plant flowers or vegetables.

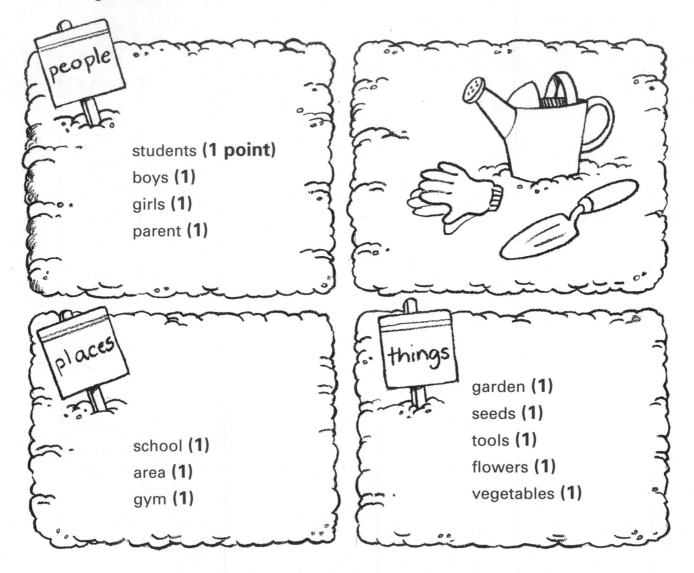

people

students (**1 point**)
boys (**1**)
girls (**1**)
parent (**1**)

places

school (**1**)
area (**1**)
gym (**1**)

things

garden (**1**)
seeds (**1**)
tools (**1**)
flowers (**1**)
vegetables (**1**)

Assessment Tip: Total **12** Points

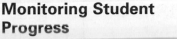

Name _____

Finding Proper Nouns

Read the sentences. Circle each proper noun.

1. (Chinese New Year) is a special holiday. **(1 point)**

2. This holiday often comes in (February) **(1)**

3. (Ryan) celebrates this holiday with his family. **(1)**

4. They invite all their relatives who live

   in (San Francisco.) **(1)**

5. Do they buy special foods from the stores on

   (Stockton Street?) **(1)**

This chart lists five common nouns. Add one proper noun for each common noun in the chart.

Answers will vary, but should be capitalized correctly.

	Common Noun	Proper Noun
people	friend	**(1 point)** _____
	teacher	**(1)** _____
places	street	**(1)** _____
	school	**(1)** _____
things	holiday	**(1)** _____

Name _____

Tricky Web of Words

Write the word that matches each clue in the puzzle.

1. a character who loves to play pranks on others
2. showing off
3. smart
4. traditional story
5. features that make a person special
6. selfish desire for more and more and more
7. bad behavior

Vocabulary

boastfulness
clever
folktale
greediness
mischief
qualities
trickster

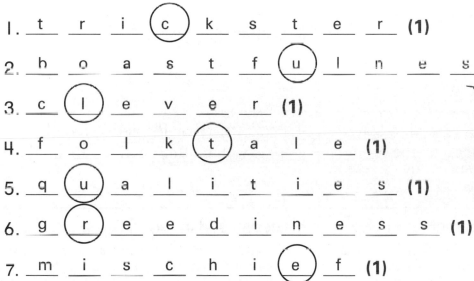

1. t r i (c) k s t e r **(1)**
2. b o a s t f (u) l n e s s **(1)**
3. c (l) e v e r **(1)**
4. f o l k (t) a l e **(1)**
5. q (u) a l i t i e s **(1)**
6. g (r) e e d i n e s s **(1)**
7. m i s c h i (e) f **(1)**

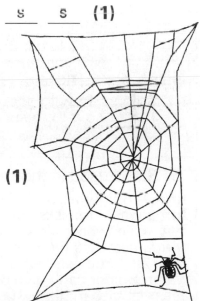

Read the letters in circles to answer the question.

What do you call the customs, beliefs, laws, and ways of living
that belong to a people?

8. (c)(u)(l)(t)(u)(r)(e) **(1)**

Name _____

Trickster Story Map

Story: "Hungry Spider"	Story: "Rabbit Races with Turtle"

1. Trickster
   Spider, Turtle **(1 point)**
	1. Trickster
	   Turtle, helped by relatives **(1)**

2. Trickster's character traits
   Spider: greedy **(1)**
   Turtle: clever **(1)**
	2. Trickster's character traits
	   clever, boastful **(1)**

3. Setting
   Spider's house; Turtle's house **(1)**
	3. Setting
	   place with four mountain ridges **(1)**

4. Problem Trickster needs to solve
   Spider: how to keep all the food;
   Turtle: how to teach Spider a lesson **(1)**
	4. Problem Trickster needs to solve
	   how to beat Rabbit in the race **(1)**

5. Steps used in the trick Trick 1: Spider asks Turtle to dinner; has Turtle wash up; asks Turtle to wash his feet, which seems in keeping with Spider's politeness; eats food while Turtle is away. Trick 2: Turtle sets out dinner under water; Spider can't dive down but then uses pebbles in his coat to sink; Turtle gets rid of him by insisting, politely, that he remove his coat; Turtle gets all the food. **(2)**	5. Steps used in the trick Turtle and Rabbit have a race; Turtle has his relatives wait at different places on the course and pretend to be him; though running fast, Rabbit appears to lose. **(2)**

6. Results
   Trick 1: Spider eats all the food;
   Trick 2: Turtle gives Spider "a taste of his own medicine." **(1)**
	6. Results
	   Turtle is named the winner. **(1)**

Assessment Tip: Total **15** Points

Name _____

It's Tricky

Compare the three trickster tales. Answers will vary.

► Draw a cover cartoon for each tale.
► Write enough about the story to make someone want to read it.

For example:

Rabbit races Turtle.
But in the end, Turtle wins!
How does slow Turtle beat
    fast Rabbit?

Aunt Fox and the Fried Fish

(4 points) _____

_____

_____

Hungry Spider

(4) _____

_____

_____

Rabbit Races with Turtle

(4) _____

_____

_____

Name _____

What Makes a Trickster Tale?

After reading each selection, complete the chart below to tell why each story is a trickster tale.

	Name the tricksters	Who was tricked?	What was the trick?
Hungry Spider	Spider, Turtle **(1 point)**	Turtle, then Spider **(1)**	Making Turtle wash his feet; making Spider eat underwater without weights **(2)**
Rabbit Races with Turtle	Turtle **(1)**	Rabbit **(1)**	A different turtle climbed over each ridge. **(2)**
Aunt Fox and the Fried Fish	Aunt Fox **(1)**	Uncle Fox, Uncle Tiger **(1)**	Making Uncle Tiger and Uncle Fox believe two different, untrue stories about each other **(2)**

Assessment Tip: Total **12** Points

Name _____

The Plot of *Aunt Fox and the Fried Fish*

Fill in the chart, using information from the trickster tale
Aunt Fox and the Fried Fish.

Problem

Aunt Fox has eaten all the fish that she was supposed to share

with Uncle Fox and Uncle Tiger. **(2 points)**

Trick

Step 1

Aunt Fox sends Uncle Fox out to sharpen knives. **(1)**

Step 2
She tells Uncle Tiger that Uncle Fox wants to cut off Uncle Tiger's
ears, so Uncle Tiger runs away. **(1)**

Step 3
She tells Uncle Fox that Uncle Tiger has left and has stolen the
fish. **(1)**

Step 4
When Uncle Fox chases Uncle Tiger, Uncle Tiger thinks he is after
his ears. Uncle Tiger runs away. **(1)**

Result

No one finds out that Aunt Fox ate all the fish. **(2)**

Assessment Tip: Total **8** Points

Name _____

Run, Rabbit, Run

Some base words take –*ed* or –*ing* endings.

walk	walk**ed**	walk**ing**
jump	jump**ed**	jump**ing**

When a base word ends in *e*, the *e* is dropped before –*ed* or –*ing*
is added.

race	rac**ed**	rac**ing**
believe	believ**ed**	believ**ing**

**Read Rabbit's description of his race. Circle each word
with an –*ed* or –*ing* ending. Then write the base words in
the box.**

I was (going) as fast as I could. But every

time I (turned) a corner, Turtle was ahead of

me. "This is (driving) me crazy!" I (shouted).

"I know I am faster than a turtle."

    I started (zooming) even faster. My feet

hardly (touched) the ground. As I (crossed) the

finish line, I (closed) my eyes. I was sure I was

the winner. I was awfully (surprised) when I

(opened) my eyes. Turtle was already there!

(10 points)

Base Words
1. go **(1 point)** _____
2. turn **(1)** _____
3. drive **(1)** _____
4. shout **(1)** _____
5. zoom **(1)** _____
6. touch **(1)** _____
7. cross **(1)** _____
8. close **(1)** _____
9. surprise **(1)** _____
10. open **(1)** _____

Assessment Tip: Total **20** Points

Name _____

The Vowel Sound in *join*

The /oi/ sound is spelled with the pattern *oi* or *oy*.

j**oi**n   j**oy**

**Write each Spelling Word under its spelling of the
/oi/ sound.** Order of answers for *oi* may vary.

oi Spelling

join **(1 point)**   point **(1)**

boil **(1)**   foil **(1)**

noise **(1)**   voice **(1)**

spoil **(1)**   coil **(1)**

choice **(1)**   broil **(1)**

soil **(1)**

oy Spelling

joy **(1)**

1. join
2. joy
3. boil
4. noise
5. spoil
6. choice
7. soil
8. point
9. foil
10. voice
11. coil
12. broil

Name _____

Spelling Spree

Use the Clue Write the Spelling Word that fits each
clue.

1. You use this to speak.
2. You can wrap food in this.
3. You might find a worm in this.
4. A pencil should have this.
5. Water does this.
6. You might hear this in a big city.

Spelling Words

1. join
2. joy
3. boil
4. noise
5. spoil
6. choice
7. soil
8. point
9. foil
10. voice
11. coil
12. broil

1. voice **(1 point)**

2. foil **(1)**

3. soil **(1)**

4. point **(1)**

5. boil **(1)**

6. noise **(1)**

Letter Math Write Spelling Words by adding and
taking away letters in the words below.

$V\cancel{ch}oice$

7. sp + oil = spoil **(1)**

8. boy – b + j = joy **(1)**

9. boil + r = broil **(1)**

10. voice – v + ch = choice **(1)**

11. coin – n + l = coil **(1)**

12. point – p + j – t = join **(1)**

Assessment Tip: Total **12** Points

Name _____

Proofreading and Writing

Proofreading Circle the five misspelled Spelling
Words in this short trickster tale. Then write each
word correctly. Order of answers may vary.

Spelling Words

1. join
2. joy
3. boil
4. noise
5. spoil
6. choice
7. soil
8. point
9. foil
10. voice
11. coil
12. broil

Wolf and Rabbit

Wolf was hungry. She put a pot of water on to
boil, but she had nothing to cook. Then she heard a
(nosie)— Rabbit was walking by her house!

"Come in and (joyn) me!" Wolf said in her
sweetest (voise). "It would be a (joi) to have
you for dinner."

"I hate to (spoyl) your plans," said Rabbit as he
leaped away, "but I think I'll let you eat alone."

1. noise **(1 point)**

2. join **(1)**

3. voice **(1)**

4. joy **(1)**

5. spoil **(1)**

Write Instructions Being a trickster takes planning. Have
you played a trick on a friend or seen someone else play a trick?
What had to be done ahead of time to prepare for the trick?

**On a separate piece of paper, write a set of instructions
that a trickster could use to play a trick. Use Spelling
Words from the list.** Responses will vary. **(5)**

Name _____

One Degree More

Daria has written a letter to her friend Eva, telling her all about her trip. But when she rereads the letter before sending it, Daria decides it is not interesting enough. Can you improve it with some strong synonyms? For each underlined word, substitute a word from the box that means the same thing, only more so. Write the synonym after the number of the word it matches

Dear Eva,

I was 1. <u>happy</u> to get your letter last month. I miss you! I hope you are not 2. <u>upset</u> with me for not writing sooner. I had a 3. <u>big</u> problem to deal with. My puppy, Mitzy, wedged her nose into a fence. I could not get her out! I pulled and pulled until I was too 4. <u>tired</u> to try anymore. Mitzy 5. <u>cried</u> so loudly the whole neighborhood came out to see what was wrong. Finally, my 6. <u>nice</u> neighbor, Ms. Gladly, cut a 7. <u>small</u> hole in the fence so we could pry Mitzy out. I had to pay for the 8. <u>damage</u> Mitzy caused. I guess it all sounds 9. <u>funny</u> now, but it was 10. <u>scary</u> at the time!

gigantic
furious
tiny
hilarious
exhausted
wonderful
delighted
destruction
terrifying
howled

Your friend,
Daria

1. <u>delighted **(1 point)**</u>

2. <u>furious **(1)**</u>

3. <u>gigantic **(1)**</u>

4. <u>exhausted **(1)**</u>

5. <u>howled **(1)**</u>

6. <u>wonderful **(1)**</u>

7. <u>tiny **(1)**</u>

8. <u>destruction **(1)**</u>

9. <u>hilarious **(1)**</u>

10. <u>terrifying **(1)**</u>

Assessment Tip: Total **10** Points

Name _____

Fixing Stringy Sentences

Correct each stringy sentence by making three simple sentences. Add periods and capital letters where they are needed.

1. This morning Uncle Fox caught three fish and the fish were big and beautiful and I fried them in the kitchen.

   This morning Uncle Fox caught three fish. The fish were big and

   beautiful. I fried them in the kitchen. **(2 points)**

2. I also cooked carrots, peas, and potatoes and there was a lot of food and so we decided to ask Uncle Tiger for lunch.

   I also cooked carrots, peas, and potatoes. There was a lot of

   food. We decided to ask Uncle Tiger for lunch. **(2)**

Correct each stringy sentence by making one simple sentence and one compound sentence. Add punctuation and capital letters where they are needed.

3. I ate all the fish myself and Uncle Tiger arrived and there was nothing to feed him.

   I ate all the fish myself. Uncle Tiger arrived, and there was

   nothing to feed him. **(2)**

4. I made up a story about Uncle Tiger and then Uncle Fox chased him and I am sorry for the trick I played.

   I made up a story about Uncle Tiger, and then Uncle Fox

   chased him. I am sorry for the trick I played. **(2)**

Name _____

Correct Sentences

Correct each stringy sentence. Make three simple sentences, or make one simple sentence and one compound sentence. Add punctuation and capital letters where needed. Answers will vary. Sample answers are given.

1. Rabbit loved to brag and Turtle loved to boast and this caused an argument.

   Rabbit loved to brag, and Turtle loved to boast. This caused

   an argument. **(2 points)**

2. Turtle and Rabbit decided to race and Rabbit was certain of winning and so he gave Turtle a lead.

   Turtle and Rabbit decided to race. Rabbit was certain of

   winning. He gave Turtle a lead. **(2)**

3. All the animals gathered for the race and some were at the starting point and others were at the end.

   All the animals gathered for the race. Some were at the

   starting point, and others were at the end. **(2)**

4. Rabbit jumped quickly to the top of the first ridge and he saw that Turtle was far ahead and so Rabbit ran even faster.

   Rabbit jumped quickly to the top of the first ridge. He saw

   that Turtle was far ahead. Rabbit ran even faster. **(2)**

5. Turtle tricked Rabbit and then Rabbit lost the race and Turtle kept his secret to himself.

   Turtle tricked Rabbit, and then Rabbit lost the race. Turtle kept

   his secret to himself. **(2)**

Assessment Tip: Total **10** Points

Name _____

More Singular/Plural Nouns

Read this script from Trickster TV Talk Show. Use proofreading marks to correct the ten errors in capitalization, end punctuation, and the spelling of plural nouns. (1 point for each correction)

Proofreading Marks

⊞	Indent
∧	Add
⌇	Delete
☰	Capital letter
/	Small letter
⊙	Add Period
∧	Add Comma
⌄⌄	Add Quotes
∿	Transpose

Example: trickster TV brings you great programes?

HOST: Today I would like to welcome our friendes Spider and Turtle. Spider, why did you invite Turtle to dinner.

SPIDER: He was very hungry

TURTLE: I certainly was, but you ate all the food. you left only the dishs.

HOST: Is that true?

SPIDER: I offered Turtle some berrys, but he left the table.
berries

TURTLE: what an unhappy time I had?

HOST: Our program for today is over. Tomorrow our guestes will be Aunt Fox and Uncle Fox. We will talk about frying fish and baking loafs of bread.
loaves

Name _____

Trickster Story Map
Answers will vary.

Characters and Setting
The Trickster and Its Character Traits **(2 points)**
Other Characters **(2)**
The Setting **(2)**

Plot
The Problem **(2)**
The Trick and the Steps Taken to Carry It Out **(2)**
The Results **(2)**

Assessment Tip: Total **12** Points

Name _____

Using Dialogue

Follow these rules when writing dialogue:

▶ Use quotation marks to enclose the spoken words. Use an end mark before the closing quotation mark if the sentence ends there. Rodney Raccoon whispered, "I'm sleepy."

▶ Use a comma before the closing quotation mark if the sentence continues. "I'm sleepy," whispered Rodney Raccoon.

Rewrite these sentences as dialogue. Use correct punctuation.

1. Rodney told Ricky that Ricky didn't know how to clean the den.

    Sample answer: "Ricky, you aren't smart enough to clean this

    den all by yourself," said Rodney. **(4 points)**

2. Ricky replied that he could clean better than anyone.

    Sample answer: Ricky replied, "That's not true! I can clean better

    than anyone." **(4)**

3. Rodney told Ricky to show that he could clean it.

    Sample answer: "You'll need to show me that you can clean,"

    said Rodney. **(4)**

4. Ricky asked Rodney what he needed to do.

    Sample answer: "What do I need to do to show you?"

    asked Ricky. **(4)**

5. Rodney replied that he would give Ricky an hour to clean.

    Sample answer: Rodney answered, " I'll give you an hour to

    clean." **(4)**

Name _____

Incredible Stories

What do you think makes a story incredible? Is it the characters, the setting, or the events? Complete the web with words or phrases that describe an incredible story.

(2 points)

(2)

(2)

Incredible
Stories

(2)

(2)

Now list some books, movies, or real events that you think are incredible. **(5)**

_____

_____

_____

_____

Name _____

Incredible Stories

Fill in the chart as you read the stories. Sample answers shown.

	What incredible thing happens?	How do the characters respond?
Dogzilla	A dog comes out of a volcano and scares a city full of mice. **(2 points)**	The mice give Dogzilla a bath. **(3)**
The Mysterious Giant of Barletta	A statue comes alive to help a town. **(2)**	The giant and the townspeople work together to trick the army. **(3)**
Raising Dragons	A dragon hatches out of an egg and is raised by a little girl. **(2)**	The little girl takes Hank to Dragon Island and comes back with more dragon eggs. **(3)**
The Garden of Abdul Gasazi	A magician turns a dog into a duck. **(2)**	Alan decides he won't be tricked again, but Miss Hester can't explain how Alan's hat got back on her porch. **(3)**

Assessment Tip: Total **20** Points

Name _____

Monster Words

Circle the two words that are most alike in meaning.

1. (colossal)
   small
   (big) **(1 point)**

2. (animal)
   (creature)
   tree **(1)**

3. strong
   (brave)
   (heroic) **(1)**

4. (huge)
   (monstrous)
   bad **(1)**

5. enormous
   (terrifying)
   (scary) **(1)**

6. (tremendous)
   tiny
   (large) **(1)**

7. (frightening)
   fun
   (horrifying) **(1)**

8. little
   (tremendous)
   (colossal) **(1)**

9. (terrifying)
   (horrifying)
   monstrous **(1)**

10. (colossal)
    heroic
    (monstrous) **(1)**

Name _____

Fantasy and Realism Chart

Sample answers provided.

Story Events and Characters	Fantasy (Make Believe)	Realism (True-to-Life)
	1. A city is built and run by mice **(1 point)** .	1. The wind carries the scent of barbecue sauce into the distance. **(1)**
	2. A monster dog attacks the mouse city. **(1)**	2. A real dog can cause trouble. **(1)**
	3. Mice send out an army. **(1)**	3. Cities have emergency meetings and emergency help, such as police officers and fire fighters. **(1)**
	4. Mice have an emergency meeting. **(1)**	4. Dogs often hate baths. **(1)**
	5. The mice chase off Dogzilla with a bath. **(1)**	5. Dogs have puppies. **(1)**

Assessment Tip: Total **10** Points

Name _____

Fix the Facts

Read this newspaper story about *Dogzilla*, and draw a line through the mistakes. Then write what really happened. Sample paragraph provided.

Monster Makes News!

The ~~people~~ in Mousopolis took part in a Cook-Off. It was ~~winter,~~ and smoke lifted over the city. Soon a strange sound was heard: "~~Quack . . . quack.~~" Then Dogzilla climbed out of a ~~cave~~!

The troops were sent out. But Dogzilla ~~hid,~~ and the troops ~~danced~~ home. Dogzilla wandered the city ~~looking for a place to sleep.~~ The mice called a meeting. The mice decided the only way to defeat Dogzilla was to think like a ~~donkey.~~ So they ~~munched grass and waited.~~ It worked! Dogzilla ran out of town. And the problem was solved ~~forever.~~

_____The **mice (1 point)** in Mousopolis took part in a Cook-off. It was **summer, (1)**

and smoke lifted over the city. Soon a strange sound was heard: **"Sniff. . . sniff." (1)**

Then Dogzilla climbed out of a **volcano. (1)**

_____The troops were sent out. But Dogzilla **breathed on the mice (1)** and the troops

ran home. **(1)** Dogzilla wandered the city **doing a lot of damage. (1)** The mice called

a meeting. The mice decided the only way to defeat Dogzilla was to think like a

dog. **(1)** So they **gave Dogzilla a bath**. **(1)** It worked! Dogzilla ran out of town.

And the problem was solved **until the Second Annual Barbecue Cook-Off. (1)**

Assessment Tip: Total **10** Points

Name _____

A Real Fantasy

**Read the story. Find parts that are fantasy
and parts that could happen in real life.**

A Fish Tale

Way up north, it's cold and dark for much of the year.
But that's how polar bears like it, or at least, that's what
people think.

"I hate the cold and dark," said Ursa Bear from her seat by
the fire. "I want to go where it's warm!"

"That's silly!" snapped her sister. "Now go catch some
fish for dinner."

Soon Ursa sat by the ocean's edge, waiting. Her first catch
was a mackerel with shiny scales.

"Please don't eat me," begged the fish. "If you let me go,
I'll grant you one wish!"

"Can you do that?" asked Ursa. "Then I wish I were
somewhere sunny and warm! Here, my friend, I'll let you go."

At once Ursa found herself on a sunny beach next to some
surprised people. "This is great!" she cried. "Now where can I
find a beach chair?"

The mackerel was even happier. "That's the tenth bear
I've wished away today!" he laughed. "Soon my fish friends
and I will be all by ourselves."

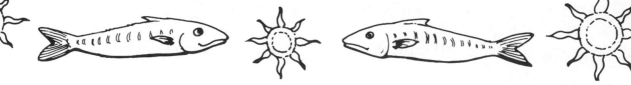

Name _____

A Real Fantasy continued

Finish the chart. List five fantasy details and five realistic details from the story.

Fantasy Details (make-believe)	Realistic Details (true-to-life)
1. polar bears who talk **(1 point)**	1. polar bears living in the far north **(1)**
2. polar bears wishing to be in a warm place **(1)**	2. cold and dark way up north **(1)**
3. a talking fish **(1)**	3. bears catching and eating fish **(1)**
4. a fish who grants wishes **(1)**	4. mackerel with shiny scales **(1)**
5. a polar bear who wants a beach chair **(1)**	5. people on a warm, sunny beach **(1)**

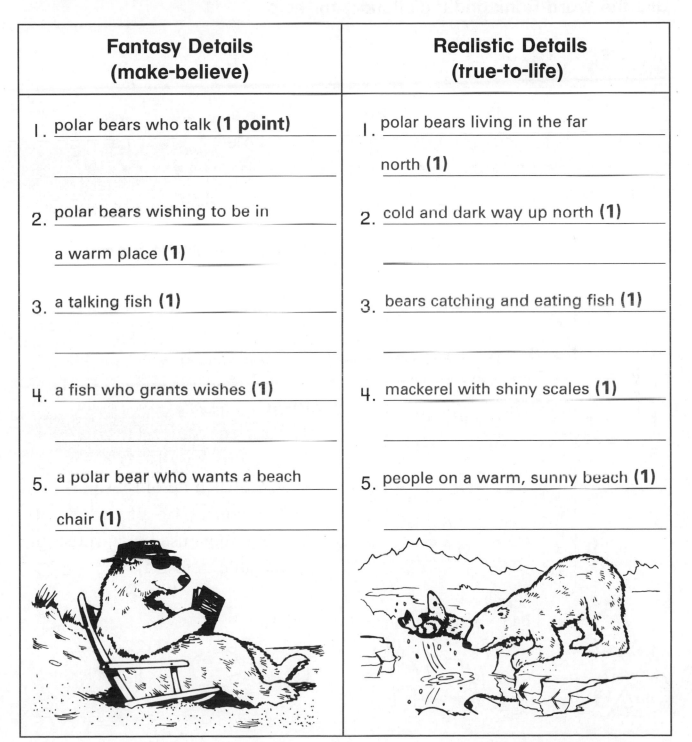

Dogzilla

Structural Analysis Forming
Plurals of Nouns Ending in
f or *fe*

Plurals Puzzle

**Write the plural noun that matches each clue in the puzzle.
Use the Word Bank and a dictionary for help.**

Word Bank

thief	cliff	life	safe	wolf
wife	calf	shelf	belief	half

Across

1. Wild animals **(1 point)**
2. Young cows **(1)**
3. Ledges to hold things **(1)**
5. People who steal **(1)**
8. Opinions **(1)**

Down

1. Married women **(1)**
2. Steep rock walls **(1)**
4. A cat has nine of these **(1)**
6. Two equal parts of a whole **(1)**
7. Containers used for protecting valuable items **(1)**

Assessment Tip: Total **10** Points

Name _____

The Vowel Sounds in *clown* and *lawn*

The /ou/ sound you hear in *clown* can be spelled with the pattern *ow* or *ou*. The /ô/ sound you hear in *lawn* can be spelled with these patterns: *aw*, *o*, or *a* before *l*.

/ou/ cl**ow**n, s**ou**nd

/ô/ l**a**wn, cl**o**th, t**a**lk

► In the starred word *would*, *ou* does not spell the /ou/ sound. Instead, *ou* spells the vowel sound you hear in the word *book*.

Write each Spelling Word under its vowel sound.

Order of answers for each category may vary.

Spelling Words

1. clown
2. lawn
3. talk
4. sound
5. cloth
6. would*
7. also
8. mouth
9. crown
10. soft
11. count
12. law

/ou/ Sound

clown **(1 point)**

sound **(1)**

mouth **(1)**

crown **(1)**

count **(1)**

/ô/ Sound

lawn **(1)**

talk **(1)**

cloth **(1)**

also **(1)**

soft **(1)**

law **(1)**

Another Vowel Sound

would **(1)**

Name _____

Spelling Spree

Hidden Words Write the Spelling Word that is
hidden in each group of letters. Do not let the
other letters fool you.

Spelling Words

1. clown
2. lawn
3. talk
4. sound
5. cloth
6. would*
7. also
8. mouth
9. crown
10. soft
11. count
12. law

   Example: e t i t o w n p e   *town*

   1. p r e s o f t a c   soft **(1 point)**

   2. c h a l s o g h e r   also **(1)**

   3. l a n r c l o t h   cloth **(1)**

   4. r e c l o w n e f   clown **(1)**

Letter Swap Change the underlined letter in each
word to make a Spelling Word. Write the Spelling
Word.

   Example: s<u>h</u>all *small*

5. cou<u>r</u>t   count **(1)**   9. tal<u>l</u>   talk **(1)**

6. <u>d</u>awn   lawn **(1)**   10. wor<u>l</u>d   would **(1)**

7. crow<u>s</u>   crown **(1)**   11. l<u>o</u>w   law **(1)**

8. <u>s</u>outh   mouth **(1)**   12. <u>m</u>ound   sound **(1)**

Assessment Tip: Total **12** Points

Name _____

Proofreading and Writing

Proofreading Circle the five misspelled Spelling
Words. Then write each word correctly.

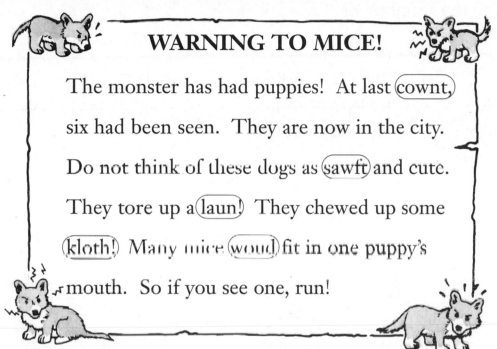

WARNING TO MICE!

The monster has had puppies! At last (cownt,)
six had been seen. They are now in the city.
Do not think of these dogs as (sawft) and cute.
They tore up a (laun!) They chewed up some
(kloth!) Many mice (woud) fit in one puppy's
mouth. So if you see one, run!

1. count **(1)**   4. cloth **(1)**

2. soft **(1)**   5. would **(1)**

3. lawn **(1)**

Write a Comparison How big is a mouse? How big
is a dog? What does a mouse eat? What does a dog
eat? How many feet does each animal have? What are
their tails like?

**On a separate piece of paper, write a comparison of
a dog and a mouse. Tell how they are alike and how
they are different. Use Spelling Words from the list.**
Responses will vary. **(5 points)**

Name _____

Find Meaning Using Context

**Choose the correct definition for each of the
underlined words in the passage. Write the letter
of the definition after the number of the word it
matches. Use context clues to help you.**

a. ran away, fled

b. frightened, alarmed

c. helpful, constructive

d. enjoyment, pleasure

e. shiver or shake

f. relating to a very
early time before
events were written
down

g. carved, as a design
on metal or glass

h. very bad, terrible

i. extremely deep place

j. call forth, gather
together

All at once, the volcano began to <u>tremble</u> and rumble. Up
from the <u>depths</u> of the earth came the <u>dreadful</u> Dogzilla! This
monster was millions of years old, from <u>prehistoric</u> times. The
mice didn't think they could teach it to do anything <u>positive</u> for
their town. Using all the courage they could <u>muster</u>, the mice
approached Dogzilla. They hit her with a blast of warm, sudsy
water. The <u>panicking</u> pooch took off at <u>top speed</u>. Delighted,
the Big Cheese watched with <u>relish</u> as Dogzilla <u>hightailed</u> it
out of town. The scary memory of the bubble bath was <u>etched</u>
in Dogzilla's mind forever.

1. e **(1)**

2. i **(1)**

3. h **(1)**

4. f **(1)**

5. c **(1)**

6. j **(1)**

7. b **(1)**

8. d **(1)**

9. a **(1)**

10. g **(1)**

Assessment Tip: Total **10** Points

Name _____

Writing Possessive Nouns

Rewrite each phrase, using a possessive.

1. the barbecue of the mouse

   the mouse's barbecue **(2 points)**

2. the behavior of the animal

   the animal's behavior **(2)**

3. the barbecue of the mice

   the mice's barbecue **(2)**

4. the shouts of the mayor

   the mayor's shouts **(2)**

5. the smoke of two volcanoes

   the two volcanoes' smoke **(2)**

6. the shouts of the citizens

   the citizens' shouts **(2)**

7. the tail of the cat

   the cat's tail **(2)**

8. the cries of the soldiers

   the soldiers' cries **(2)**

9. the dog belonging to the Smiths

   the Smiths' dog **(2)**

10. the dog belonging to Abigail

    Abigail's dog **(2)**

Name _____

Finding the Possessive

On the line provided, write the noun in parentheses as a possessive noun to complete each sentence. Then write *S* if the possessive noun is singular, and *P* if it is plural.

1. The ___artist's **(2 points)**___ pictures dazzle the reader. (artist) __S__

2. I think that the ___readers' **(2)**___ interest will be high. (readers) __P__

3. An ___illustrator's **(2)**___ imagination is clear on every page. (illustrator) __S__

4. The ___dog's **(2)**___ expression looks like a smile. (dog) __S__

5. At the end of the story, the ___puppies' **(2)**___ faces are adorable. (puppies) __P__

6. Most ___monsters' **(2)**___ faces aren't that cute! (monsters) __P__

7. Every ___reader's **(2)**___ reaction will be a little different. (reader) __S__

8. All of the ___characters' **(2)**___ actions were ridiculous. (characters) __P__

9. I think that our ___class's **(2)**___ favorite character is Dogzilla. (class) __S__

10. The book was awarded a prize by the ___teachers' **(2)**___ committee. (teachers) __P__

Assessment Tip: Total **20** Points

Name _____

Apostrophes

Rewrite each of the following sentences, adding apostrophes to each incorrectly spelled possessive noun.

1. How would Dav Pilkeys book be different if it were called *Frogzilla*?

   How would Dav Pilkey's book be different if it were called *Frogzilla*? _____

   (2 points) _____

2. The city would be crushed by Frogzillas huge feet.

   The city would be crushed by Frogzilla's huge feet. **(2)** _____

   _____

3. The new heros name might be Dennis the Fly.

   The new hero's name might be Dennis the Fly. **(2)** _____

   _____

4. What do you think the flys strategy would be?

   What do you think the fly's strategy would be? **(2)** _____

   _____

5. What are the frogs weaknesses?

   What are the frogs' weaknesses? **(2)** _____

   _____

Name _____

Writing a Journal Entry

**In the space below, write a journal entry for today.
Describe things you see, feel, think about, or remember.
Then use your entry to complete the table below.**

My Daily Journal

Today's Date: _____

Journal entries will vary. **(5 points)**

_____
_____
_____
_____
_____
_____
_____
_____

What I Wrote About Today

Facts	Observations	Feelings	Memories	Ideas
Entries will vary. (2)	Entries will vary. (2)	Entries will vary. (2)	Entries will vary. (2)	Entries will vary. (2)

Assessment Tip: Total **15** Points

Name _____

Voice

Suppose one of the puppies wrote this journal entry:

Those silly mice! They think their big barbecue (tommorow) will

go off without a hitch. Well, they've had their peace and quiet.

Now let's see if they like to play with (puppys!) I'm raring to go,

and I'm planning on having lots of fun in Mousopolis tomorrow.

And if they (tries) any of that bath stuff on me, we'll just see who

can take a licking!

Suppose the Big Cheese wrote this in his journal:

Tomorrow is the first anniversary of the Dogzilla disaster, and

that makes me nervous. What (hapened) to Dogzilla? Can we be

sure she (don't) come back? Will tomorrow be the day a new

monster (destroies) poor Mousopolis yet again? I'm scared!

1. How would you describe the puppy's voice in his entry?

   The puppy is excited and self-confident and is looking forward to

   tomorrow with glee. **(2 points)**

2. How would you describe the Big Cheese's voice in his entry?

   The Big Cheese is worried and frightened and is looking forward to

   tomorrow with dread. **(2)**

**In both journal entries, circle examples of grammar and
spelling that are not perfect.** See circled items in the journal entries. **(2)**

Name _____

Revising Your Story

Reread your story. Put a checkmark in the box for each sentence that describes your paper. Use this page to help you revise.

Rings the Bell

☐ My story has a beginning, a middle, and an ending. It is focused on a clear problem.

☐ Many details tell about the characters and setting.

☐ Exact words make a clear picture for the reader.

☐ I wrote in a way that will get my readers' attention.

☐ Sentences flow well. There are few mistakes.

Getting Stronger

☐ The beginning or ending is confusing. The problem is unclear.

☐ I need more details about my characters and my setting.

☐ More exact words are needed.

☐ My writing doesn't always hold my readers' attention.

☐ Some sentences are choppy. There are some mistakes.

Try Harder

☐ There is no beginning, middle, or ending. There is no problem.

☐ I didn't use any details.

☐ There are no exact words. I used the same word many times.

☐ I can't hear my voice at all. My readers might be bored.

☐ Most sentences are choppy. Mistakes make it hard to read.

Name _____

Using Possessive Nouns

A **possessive noun** shows ownership.

► Add *'s* to make a noun possessive.

► Add just an ' (apostrophe) to make a plural noun that ends with *s* a possessive noun.

Rewrite each phrase, using a possessive noun. Then use the new phrase in a sentence of your own. Sentences will vary.

1. the equipment of the team the team's equipment **(2 points)**

   _____

   _____

2. the teamwork of the players the players' teamwork **(2)**

   _____

   _____

3. the orders of the coach the coach's orders **(2)**

   _____

   _____

4. the roar of the audience the audience's roar **(2)**

   _____

   _____

5. the songs of the cheerleaders the cheerleaders' songs **(2)**

   _____

   _____

Name _____

Spelling Words

Look for spelling patterns you have learned to help you remember the Spelling Words on this page. Think about the parts that you find hard to spell.

Write the missing letters in the Spelling Words below.

Spelling Words

1. and
2. said
3. goes
4. going
5. some
6. something
7. you
8. your
9. friend
10. school
11. where
12. myself

1. an <u>d</u>____ **(1 point)**

2. s <u>a</u>____ <u>i</u>____ d **(1)**

3. go <u>e</u>____ <u>s</u>____ **(1)**

4. go <u>i</u>____ n ____ <u>g</u>____ **(1)**

5. s <u>o</u>____ me **(1)**

6. som <u>e</u>____ thing **(1)**

7. y <u>o</u>____ <u>u</u>____ **(1)**

8. y <u>o</u>____ u ____ <u>r</u>____ **(1)**

9. fr <u>i</u>____ <u>e</u>____ nd **(1)**

10. s <u>c</u>____ <u>h</u>____ ool **(1)**

11. w <u>h</u>____ ere **(1)**

12. m <u>y</u>____ <u>s</u>____ elf **(1)**

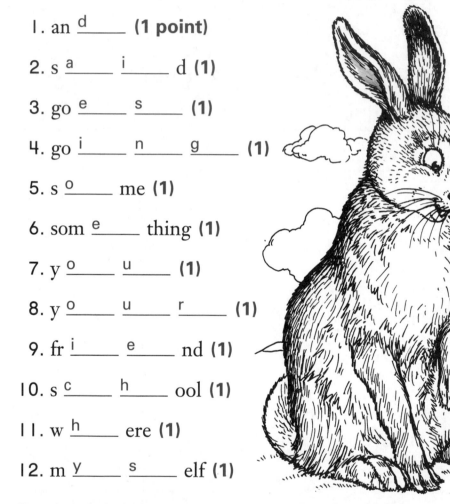

Study List On another sheet of paper, write each Spelling Word. Check the list to be sure you spell each word correctly. Order of words may vary. **(2)**

Name _____

Spelling Spree

The Third Word Write the Spelling Word that belongs in each group.

1. I, me,   myself **(1 point)** _____

2. plus, also,   and **(1)** _____

3. talked, spoke,   said **(1)** _____

4. pal, buddy,   friend **(1)** _____

5. their, our,   your **(1)** _____

6. moves, runs,   goes **(1)** _____

Sentence Fillers Write the Spelling Word that makes the most sense in each sentence below.

7. Do you know where **(1)** _____ soccer practice is tomorrow?

8. I have some **(1)** _____ books about bears that I bought last summer.

9. Our school **(1)** _____ usually lets out at 3 o'clock.

10. When is your class going **(1)** _____ to the library?

11. My brother wrote something **(1)** _____ in my notebook, but I can't read it.

12. Have you **(1)** _____ seen my pet snake anywhere?

Spelling Words

1. and
2. said
3. goes
4. going
5. some
6. something
7. you
8. your
9. friend
10. school
11. where
12. myself

Theme 3: **Incredible Stories**   213
Assessment Tip: Total **12** Points

Proofreading and Writing

Proofreading Circle the four misspelled Spelling Words in the story. Then write each word correctly.

Yesterday, I was on my way into (skool) when I heard something rustling in the bushes. I turned around (an) went over to see what it was. I looked in the spot (were) I had heard the noise, but there was nothing there. Then, from behind me, a voice (sed), "Are you looking for me?" I turned around and found myself face to face with a fox with a sly grin on its face.

Spelling Words

1. and
2. said
3. goes
4. going
5. some
6. something
7. you
8. your
9. friend
10. school
11. where
12. myself

1. school **(2 points)**   3. where **(2)**
2. and **(2)**   4. said **(2)**

✏️ **Incredible Sentences** Write four sentences that tell about **something incredible**. Use a Spelling Word from the list in each one. Sentences will vary. **(4)**

214   Theme 3: **Incredible Stories**
Assessment Tip: Total **12** Points

Name _____

What Do These Words Mean?

Look up each word in your glossary. Then, in the box above each word, draw a picture that shows the meaning of the word.

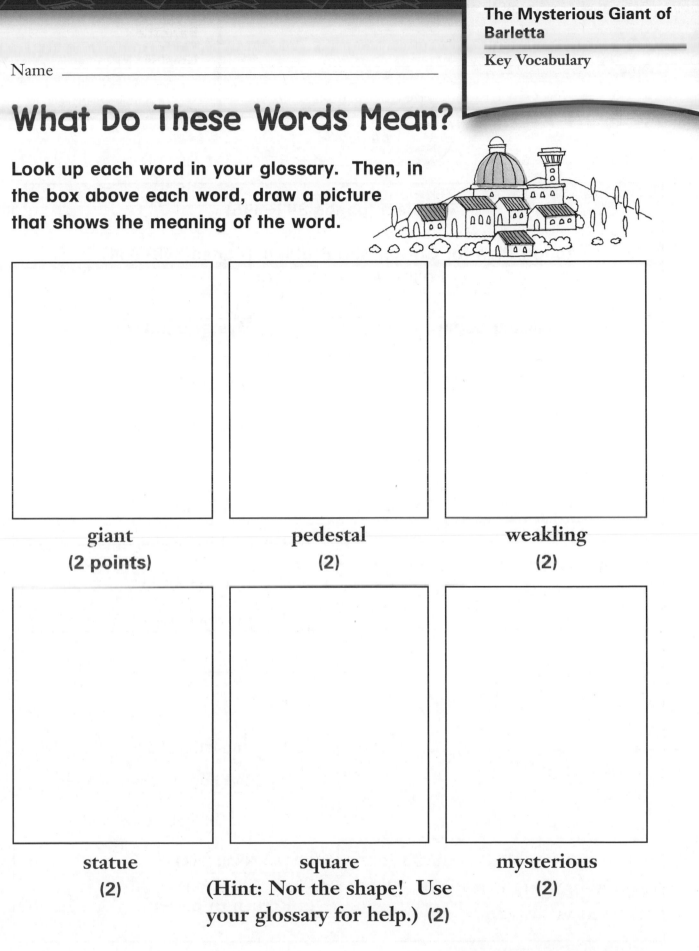

giant
(2 points)

pedestal
(2)

weakling
(2)

statue
(2)

square
(Hint: Not the shape! Use
your glossary for help.) (2)

mysterious
(2)

Name _____

Action Plan

Problem (pages 344–345)	
Action Plan for Solving the Problem (pages 348–354) **Follow these directions:**	
Townspeople	**Mysterious Giant**
1. Find an <u>onion **(1 point)**</u> .	1. Take the <u>onion halves **(1)**</u> from Zia Concetta.
2. <u>Hide yourselves. **(1)**</u>	
3. Don't ask <u>any questions **(1)**</u> _____ .	2. <u>Step down from the pedestal. **(1)**</u> _____
	3. Travel three miles outside the city and <u>sit down **(1)**</u> .
	4. <u>Hold the onion halves close to</u> <u>your eyes, make sobbing noises,</u> <u>and cry. **(2)**</u>
	5. Tell the army that <u>the other boys in town pick on</u> <u>you and call you "tiny" and a</u> <u>"weakling." **(2)**</u>
	6. Return to Barletta.

Assessment Tip: Total **10** Points

Name _____

Remember the Details

Think about *The Mysterious Giant of Barletta*. Then complete the sentences.

1. The people of Barletta show their love for the Mysterious Giant by

    greeting him, asking him for good luck, playing near him, and, for older boys

    and girls, spending time near him. **(2 points)**

2. The peaceful time for Barletta is over when

    word reaches the town that a large army is on its way. **(2)**

3. Zia Concetta and the Giant figure out a plan to save Barletta. The plan is

    for the Giant to use onion pieces to make himself cry. He must tell the soldiers

    that he's crying because the other boys pick on him since he's so small. **(2)**

4. After the soldiers hear what the Giant says, they wonder

    how big the rest of the townspeople are. **(2)**

5. The army captain decides there is only one thing to do, so they

    turn around and run in the opposite direction of Barletta. **(2)**

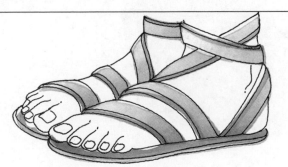

Name _____

Directions for Fun

Read the directions. Then answer the questions on the next page.

Fingertip Puppets

Act out your favorite folktale or story using puppets you've made yourself. It's easy and fun to do. All you need are an old rubber glove, scissors, glue, marking pens, and some craft supplies.

First, find an old rubber glove that can be cut apart. Each finger will become a puppet. Draw a line about 2 ½ inches below each fingertip of the glove. Cut along the line and then turn the fingertip inside out.

Next, make the puppet look special. Draw a funny face on your puppet. Then glue on hair made from cotton or yarn. Finally, glue on a hat, shirt, or collar made with pieces of felt. You may also want to add beads, buttons, or trims.

Name _____

Directions for Fun continued

Answer each question about making a fingertip puppet.

1. What supplies will you need?

   An old rubber glove, scissors, glue, marking pens, and craft supplies

   like yarn or cotton, felt, beads, buttons, and trims. **(2 points)**

2. After you find an old rubber glove, what do you do?

   Draw a line 2 ½ inches below each fingertip. **(2)**

3. Why should you draw the line before you cut?

   The line shows you where to cut. **(2)**

4. After you cut off the fingertip, what should you do next?

   Turn the fingertip inside out. **(2)**

5. What should you do before you glue on the hair?

   Draw the face. **(2)**

Name _____

Giant Endings

Fill in each blank using the base word and the ending -*er* or
-*est*. The base words are in dark type. To solve the puzzle,
write the numbered letter from each answer on the line with
the matching number.

1. The statue was the t a l l e s t thing
                     5

   in Barletta. **(tall) (1 point)**

2. The statue had been in the square l o n g e r
                                    7

   than anyone could remember. **(long) (1)**

3. To the Giant, late nights were the n i c e s t
                                 1

   time of all. **(nice) (1)**

4. The town was q u i e t e r at night
                 3

   than at any other time. **(quiet) (1)**

5. The army was s t r o n g e r than
                  2   6

   the people of Barletta. **(strong) (1)**

6. The torches were b r i g h t e r
                           4

   than ever. **(bright) (1)**

The Mysterious Giant has a lot of:

c o u r a g e
1 2 3 4 5 6 7

Assessment Tip: Total **6** Points

Name _____

Vowel + /r/ Sounds

Remember these spelling patterns for the vowel + /r/ sounds:

Patterns		Examples
/är/	**ar**	dark
/îr/	**ear**	clear
/ôr/	**or**	north
/ûr/	**er**	her
	ir	girl
	ur	turn
	or	work

1. girl
2. clear
3. her
4. turn
5. dark
6. work
7. smart
8. word
9. hurt
10. serve
11. north
12. third

Write each Spelling Word under its vowel + /r/ sounds. Order of answers for each category may vary.

/är/ Sounds
dark **(1 point)**

smart **(1)**

/îr/ Sounds
clear **(1)**

/ôr/ Sounds
north **(1)**

/ûr/ Sounds
girl **(1)**

her **(1)**

work **(1)**

word **(1)**

serve **(1)**

third **(1)**

turn **(1)**

hurt **(1)**

Assessment Tip: Total **12** Points

Name _____

Spelling Spree

Questions Write a Spelling Word to answer each question.

1. What direction is opposite to south?
2. How do you feel when you solve a hard problem?
3. What might a car do at a street corner?
4. What do you call a sky without clouds?
5. What is it like outside after sunset?
6. What comes between second and fourth?

1. girl
2. clear
3. her
4. turn
5. dark
6. work
7. smart
8. word
9. hurt
10. serve
11. north
12. third

1. north **(1 point)**
2. smart **(1)**
3. turn **(1)**
4. clear **(1)**
5. dark **(1)**
6. third **(1)**

Missing Letters Each missing letter fits in ABC order between the other letters. Write the missing letters to spell a Spelling Word.

Example: g __ i n __ p q __ s m __ o *horn*

7. r __ t d __ f q __ s u __ w d __ f   serve **(1 point)**
8. g __ i d __ f q __ s   her **(1)**
9. v __ x n __ p q __ s j __ l   work **(1)**
10. f __ h h __ j q __ s k __ m   girl **(1)**
11. v __ x n __ p q __ s c __ e   word **(1)**
12. g __ i t __ v q __ s s __ u   hurt **(1)**

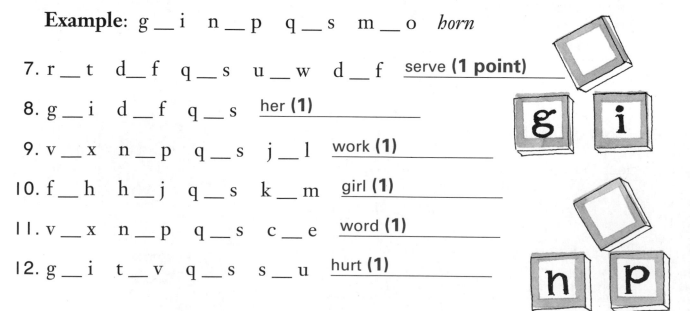

222   Theme 3: **Incredible Stories**
Assessment Tip: Total **12** Points

Name _____

Proofreading and Writing

Proofreading Circle the four misspelled Spelling Words below. Then write each word correctly.

Here is a good way to reach Barletta. Head (noarth) from Naples. At the edge of town, turn right onto the main highway. This road should be pretty (cleer.) Take the (therd) exit after you reach the coast. You should get to Barletta before (darck.)

Spelling Words

1. girl
2. clear
3. her
4. turn
5. dark
6. work
7. smart
8. word
9. hurt
10. serve
11. north
12. third

north **(1 point)** _____   third **(1)** _____

clear **(1)** _____   dark **(1)** _____

Write a Description If you were to make a statue, who would be your subject? Where would it stand so others could see it?

On a separate sheet of paper, write a description of your statue. Tell where it will be placed. Use Spelling Words from the list. Responses will vary. **(4 points)**

Which Meaning Is Correct?

From the definitions below, choose the correct meaning for the underlined word in each sentence. Write the number of the meaning in the blank provided.

---

bargain *noun* **1.** An agreement between two sides; deal: *We made a bargain to split the chores.* **2.** Something offered or bought at a low price: *The book was a bargain at 25 cents.*

---

hail *verb* **1.** To greet or welcome by calling out: *We hailed our friends as they got off the bus.* **2.** To call or signal to: *I hailed a taxi at the corner* **3.** To congratulate by cheering: *The crowd hailed the hero's return.*

---

settle *verb* **1.** To arrange or decide upon: *Let's settle the argument today.* **2.** To come to rest: *The leaf settled on the grass.* **3.** To make a home or place to live in: *Pioneers settled on the prairie.*

---

1. Every day, the townspeople <u>hailed</u> the Mysterious Giant as they walked to the market. <u>1 **(2 points)**</u>

2. They asked the statue to help them find a good <u>bargain</u> at the market. <u>2 **(2)**</u>

3. Doves flew to the statue and <u>settled</u> on his head. <u>2 **(2)**</u>

4. The Mysterious Giant was <u>hailed</u> as a hero. <u>3 **(2)**</u>

Assessment Tip: Total **8** Points

Name _____

Circling Verbs

Circle the verb in each sentence.

1. The giant statue (stands) in the center of town. **(1 point)**

2. People often (look) at the statue. **(1)**

3. Everyone (loves) the statue. **(1)**

4. Zia Concetta (is) the oldest person in Barletta. **(1)**

5. One day, an enemy army (approaches) the town. **(1)**

6. Everyone (fears) the army of powerful soldiers. **(1)**

7. The soldiers (march) toward the town. **(1)**

8. The mysterious statue (hops) off his pedestal. **(1)**

9. He (asks) for three special things. **(1)**

10. The giant statue (cries) because of the onion's smell. **(1)**

Name _____

Finding Verbs

Find the verb in each sentence, and write it on the line at the right.

1. In this story, the giant statue leaps off its pedestal. <u>leaps</u> **(1 point)** _____

2. The people believe in the giant. <u>believe</u> **(1)** _____

3. Clearly, the giant cares about the town of Barletta. <u>cares</u> **(1)** _____

4. Unfortunately, an army attacks the town. <u>attacks</u> **(1)** _____

5. The people quickly identify the trouble. <u>identify</u> **(1)** _____

6. With a little thought, the giant solves the problem. <u>solves</u> **(1)** _____

7. He cuts an onion into two pieces. <u>cuts</u> **(1)** _____

8. The tears run down his face. <u>run</u> **(1)** _____

9. The army fears the giant and his friends. <u>fears</u> **(1)** _____

10. At the end of the story, the soldiers leave town. <u>leave</u> **(1)** _____

Use this chart to classify the verbs from the sentences above.

Physical Action	Mental Action
leaps **(1)**	believe **(1)**
attacks **(1)**	cares **(1)**
cuts **(1)**	identify **(1)**
run **(1)**	solves **(1)**
leave **(1)**	fears **(1)**

Assessment Tip: Total **20** Points

Name _____

Using Exact Verbs

Circle the verb in each sentence. Then think of an exact verb to make the sentence more interesting. Rewrite the sentence using your exact verb. Student's verb choices will vary. Possible responses given.

1. An army of powerful soldiers appears.

   An army of powerful soldiers **attacks**. **(2 points)** _____

2. One night, Zia Concetta goes to the statue.

   One night, Zia Concetta **rushes** to the statue. **(2)** _____

3. The giant statue moves off the pedestal.

   The giant statue **leaps** off the pedestal. **(2)** _____

4. The statue's clever plan beats the large army.

   The statue's clever plan **outsmarts** the large army. **(2)** _____

5. Today, the statue still is in Barletta, Italy.

   Today, the statue still **stands** in Barletta, Italy. **(2)** _____

Theme 3: **Incredible Stories**   227
Assessment Tip: Total **10 Points**

Name _____

Write a Thank-You Note

Use this outline to write a thank-you letter for a gift you have been given. When you have finished your letter, answer the questions below. Responses will vary.

Address/Date **(2 points)**
_____
_____
_____

Greeting **(2)** _____

Body

Students should name the gift in the first sentence. **(2)**

Students should tell why they enjoyed receiving and using the gift.

(2) _____
_____
_____

Closing **(2)** _____

Signature **(2)** _____

What did you say in your letter to explain why the gift is important to you?

Responses will vary. **(2)**
_____
_____

What did you say in your letter to make the giver feel good about giving the gift?

Responses will vary. **(2)**
_____
_____

Assessment Tip: Total **16** Points

Name _____

Using Commas for Direct Address

What if in all the excitement at Barletta, no one remembered to thank the vegetable store owner for supplying the very important onion?

Suppose that the thank-you note has now been written, but it needs proofreading. Read the note. Add commas where they belong, before or after the name of the person being addressed.

(Each comma in the letter is worth **2 points**.)

Dear Sir,

We the people of Barletta thank you for supplying the onion that made our giant cry! Sir, without your onion, our whole plan might have failed miserably. We were ready to run from Barletta, but you, Sir, stayed bravely in your shop, guarding your vegetables. When your city needed you, you were ready, Sir. When we said, "Sir, find us an onion," you knew just what to do. Now everyone will always say that it was because of you and your onion that Barletta was saved. Sir, you have reason to be proud!

Sincerely,
The Mayor

Name _____

Farm Words

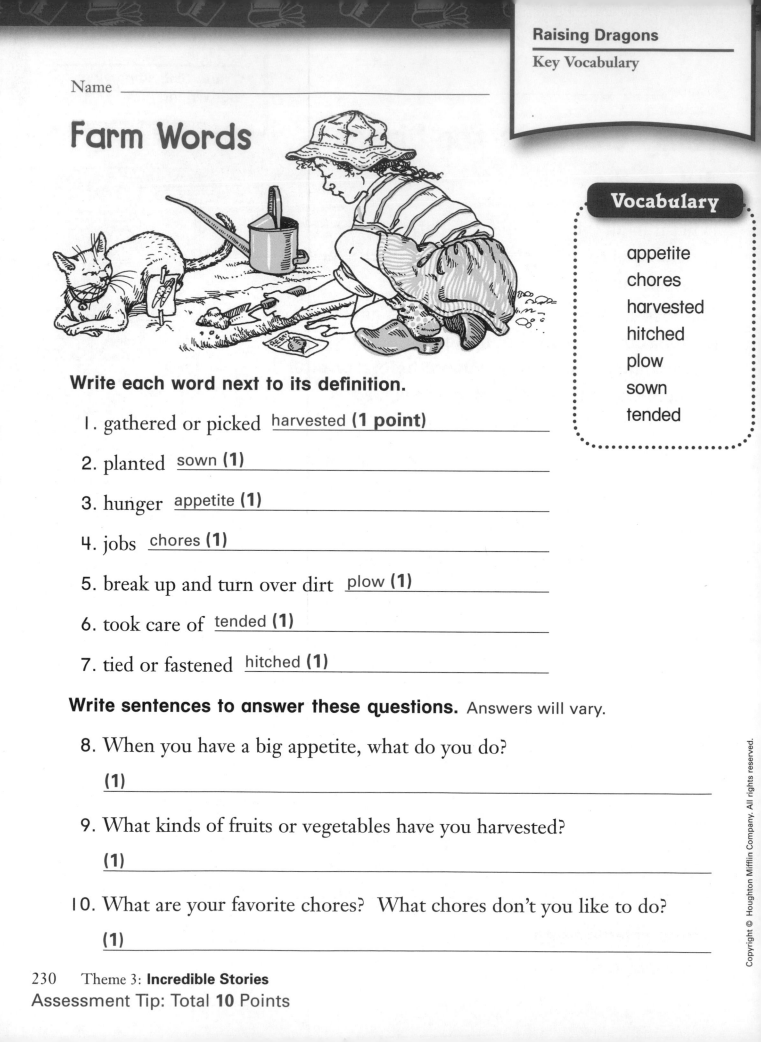

Write each word next to its definition.

1. gathered or picked <u>harvested **(1 point)**</u>

2. planted <u>sown **(1)**</u>

3. hunger <u>appetite **(1)**</u>

4. jobs <u>chores **(1)**</u>

5. break up and turn over dirt <u>plow **(1)**</u>

6. took care of <u>tended **(1)**</u>

7. tied or fastened <u>hitched **(1)**</u>

Write sentences to answer these questions. Answers will vary.

8. When you have a big appetite, what do you do?

   <u>**(1)**</u>

9. What kinds of fruits or vegetables have you harvested?

   <u>**(1)**</u>

10. What are your favorite chores? What chores don't you like to do?

   <u>**(1)**</u>

Assessment Tip: Total **10** Points

Name _____

Conclusions Chart

Sample responses are provided.

Story Details		Story Details		Conclusion
(page 366) Pa raises corn, peas, barley, wheat, and many farm animals.	+	(Page 366) He says he has no time for make believe. **(1 point)**	=	Pa works hard on the farm. **(1)**
(page 369; it's not a rock.) It's too round, smooth and not hard enough. **(1 point)**	+	(page 371) A tiny dragon hatches from it. **(1)**	=	(What's in Miller's Cave) a dragon egg **(1)**
(page 374; Hank's size) Hank grows to be as big as a barn from tail to snout. **(1)**	+	(Page 374) Hank has wings. **(1)**	=	(What Hank looks like) extraordinary; unusual **(2)**
(page 380) He starts drawing crowds and attention. **(2)**	+	(page 383) Hank feels right at home on the island. **(2)**	=	(Hank's fate) He's better off living on the dragon-shaped island. **(2)**

Assessment Tip: Total **15** Points

Name _____

The Dragon's Tale

Tell what happened in *Raising Dragons*.
Complete each sentence to finish the story.
Sample answers are provided.

One day a little girl found what looked like a big rock. It was

an egg. She kept wondering <u>what was coming out of the egg. **(1 point)**</u>

_____ .

One night she heard <u>a loud noise **(1)**</u> .

Then the little girl saw <u>a tiny dragon **(1)**</u> .

Of course, the girl loved Hank. Each day she fed him and

<u>took care of him **(1)**</u> .

Soon he was part of their lives.

Hank helped around the farm. He saved Ma's tomatoes. He

also saved the corn by <u>setting fire to the field and making popcorn. **(1)**</u>

_____ .

Then Hank got too much attention. So the girl took Hank to

<u>a dragon-shaped island **(1)**</u> . She knew

Hank could live there because <u>he got along well with the other</u>

<u>dragons **(1)**</u>

But Hank surprised the little girl with <u>more dragon eggs to take</u>

<u>home **(1)**</u>

232   Theme 3: **Incredible Stories**
Assessment Tip: Total **8** Points

Name _____

Conclusions from Clues

Read these details about dragons. Then fill in the chart on the next page.

What Dragons Are Really Like

► Dragons have skin much like snakes, lizards, and other reptiles. Since they are cold-blooded, dragons like to live in warm spots.

► Each spring, dragons lay eggs in nests they build. Their nests are made from the same materials that birds use.

► Dragons can fly, but their wings are not at all like birds' wings. They are more like large, leathery bat wings.

► Usually, dragons will not harm people. They only eat frogs, bugs, and fish. Some dragons have been trained to be useful. They pull plows and do other tasks that horses do.

► Dragons do not breathe fire. However, their teeth are larger than a shark's, and they will use them to keep their babies safe.

Name _____

Conclusions from Clues continued

Read each conclusion. Decide if it is correct, and write YES or NO. Write the clues that helped you decide.

Conclusions	Correct Conclusion? (Yes or No)	Story Clues
Dragon skin is scaly.	Yes **(1 point)**	Their skin is much like that of a snake's or lizard's. **(2)**
Dragon nests are made of twigs, sticks, and grasses.	Yes **(1)**	Their nests are made from the same materials that birds use. **(2)**
Dragon wings have feathers.	No **(1)**	Their wings are not like birds' wings. They are more like large, leathery bat wings. **(2)**
Dragons can be trained to carry riders.	Yes **(1)**	They can be trained to do things that horses can do. **(2)**
Dragons never bite.	No **(1)**	They will use their teeth to keep their babies safe. **(2)**

Assessment Tip: Total **15** Points

Name _____

Happy Endings

Choose a word from the box to match each picture clue.
Write the word on the line.

Word Bank

proudly	brightly	leaky	cloudy	beastly
furry	lovely	bumpy	rainy	hairy

1. + y = r a i n y **(1 point)**

2. + ly = b r i g h t l y **(1)**

3. + y = c l o u d y **(1)**

4. + ly = b e a s t l y **(1)**

5. + y = b u m p y **(1)**

6. + ly = l o v e l y **(1)**

Name _____

The /j/, /k/, and /kw/ Sounds

▶ The /j/ sound can be spelled with the consonant *j* or with the consonant *g* followed by *e* or *y*.

/j/ **j**eans, lar**ge**, **gy**m

▶ The starred word *judge* has two /j/ sounds in it. The first /j/ sound is spelled *j*, and the second is spelled *dge*.

▶ The /k/ sound can be spelled with *k*, *ck*, or *c*. The /kw/ sounds can be spelled with the *qu* pattern.

/k/ par**k**, qui**ck**, pi**c**nic   /kw/ **squ**eeze

Write the Spelling Words that have the /j/ sound in them. Then write the Spelling Words that have the /k/ or /kw/ sounds in them.

Spelling Words:

1. large
2. gym
3. skin
4. quick
5. picnic
6. judge
7. park
8. jeans
9. crack
10. orange
11. second
12. squeeze

/j/ Sound

large **(1 point)**

gym **(1)**

judge **(1)**

jeans **(1)**

orange **(1)**

/k/ or /kw/ Sounds

skin **(1)**

quick **(1)**

picnic **(1)**

park **(1)**

crack **(1)**

second **(1)**

squeeze **(1)**

Assessment Tip: Total **12** Points

Name _____

Spelling Spree

Silly Rhymes Write a Spelling Word to complete each sentence. The answer rhymes with the underlined word.

1. large
2. gym
3. skin
4. quick
5. picnic
6. judge
7. park
8. jeans
9. crack
10. orange
11. second
12. squeeze

1. The hungry _____ ate some <u>fudge</u>.

2. Birds in the _____ sleep after <u>dark</u>.

3. I dropped baked <u>beans</u> on my new _____ .

4. There is a _____ in the train <u>track</u>.

5. Can more bees _____ into the <u>hive</u>?

6. A _____ <u>barge</u> is on the river.

1. judge **(1 point)**   4. crack **(1)**

2. park **(1)**   5. squeeze **(1)**

3. jeans **(1)**   6. large **(1)**

Letter Math Solve each problem by using a Spelling Word.

Example: joke – ke + b = *job*

7. pick – k + nic = picnic **(1)**

8. or + angel – l = orange **(1)**

9. s + king – g = skin **(1)**   11. sec + fond – f = second **(1)**

10. quit – t + ck = quick **(1)**   12. edgy – ed + m = gym **(1)**

Assessment Tip: Total **12** Points

Name _____

Proofreading and Writing

Proofreading Circle the five misspelled Spelling Words. Then write each word correctly.

1. large
2. gym
3. skin
4. quick
5. picnic
6. judge
7. park
8. jeans
9. crack
10. orange
11. second
12. squeeze

Dear Diary,

Today we went to the zoo. We saw (larje) snakes and turtles. One turtle splashed water on my (geans!) There was a dragon cage, but it was empty. I guess the dragons were taking a (quik) nap inside. For lunch we had a (picnick) I ate mine in the (parc.)

1. large **(1 point)**

2. jeans **(1)**

3. quick **(1)**

4. picnic **(1)**

5. park **(1)**

Write a List of Rules A baby dragon would need a lot of care. What rules should someone follow when raising a dragon?

On a separate sheet of paper, write a list of rules for taking care of a dragon. Use Spelling Words from the list.

Responses will vary. **(5)**

Assessment Tip: Total **10** Points

Name _____

Say It Right!

Pronunciation Key			
ă map	ĭ pit	oi **oil**	th **bath**
ā pay	ī ride	o͝o book	_th_ **bathe**
â care	î **fierce**	o͞o boot	ə ago, item,
ä father	ŏ pot	ou **out**	pencil, atom,
ĕ pet	ō go	ŭ cup	circus
ē be	ô paw, for	û fur	

**Look at the vowel sound in the words below. Then look at
the Pronunciation Key and find the sample word with the
same vowel sound. Write the word on the line.**

1. **must** (mŭst) cup **(1 point)**

2. **dirt** (dûrt) fur **(1)**

3. **breath** (brĕth) pet **(1)**

4. **path** (păth) map **(1)**

5. **chew** (cho͞o) boot **(1)**

6. **self** (sĕlf) pet **(1)**

7. **dear** (dîr) fierce **(1)**

8. **pair** (pâr) care **(1)**

9. **meal** (mēl) be **(1)**

10. **stay** (stā) pay **(1)**

Name _____

Looking for the Present

Read each sentence. Choose the correct verb form and write it on the line to complete the sentence.

1. This story __tells **(1 point)**__ about a girl and her pet dragon. (tell   tells)

2. The dog __barks **(1)**__ when it sees the giant egg. (barks   bark)

3. The neighbors __watch **(1)**__ the egg hatching. (watch   watches)

4. A large claw __appears **(1)**__ from inside the egg. (appear   appears)

5. The girl __dries **(1)**__ the newborn dragon. (dry   dries)

6. The strange pet __smiles **(1)**__ when he sees the girl. (smiles   smile)

7. Her parents __worry **(1)**__ about owning a dragon. (worries   worry)

8. Dragons __breathe **(1)**__ fire. (breathe   breathes)

9. The dragon __flies **(1)**__ with the girl on his back. (flies fly)

10. Clouds __surround **(1)**__ the two flying friends. (surround surrounds)

Assessment Tip: Total **10** Points

Name _____

Choosing the Present

Read each sentence. Then write the correct present-time form of the verb in parentheses.

1. A smart girl _raises_ **(1)** _____ a pet dragon. (raise)

2. The chickens _cluck_ **(1)** _____ when they see the baby dragon. (cluck)

3. All animals _need_ **(1)** _____ to eat. (need)

4. This dragon _munches_ **(1)** _____ on fish, frogs, eels, and insects. (munch)

5. The strange creature _tries_ **(1)** _____ to be a good friend. (try)

6. The friends _cross_ **(1)** _____ the farm together. (cross)

7. The dragon _helps_ **(1)** _____ with daily chores. (help)

8. His hot breath _pops_ **(1)** _____ the corn in the field. (pop)

9. Customers _buy_ **(1)** _____ the dragon's popcorn. (buy)

10. The girl _cries_ **(1)** _____ when the dragon leaves. (cry)

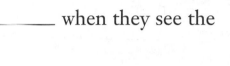

Theme 3: **Incredible Stories**   241
Assessment Tip: Total **10** Points

Name _____

Subject-Verb Agreement

**Proofread these paragraphs. Correct
errors in subject-verb agreement.
Circle verbs that are not in the correct time.
Then rewrite the paragraphs on the lines provided.** Each word
is **1 point**.

Benjamin wakes at sunrise. He (look) outside his apartment window. At first, he (see) only the sun. Then he (spot) five black dots in the distance. The dots (grows) bigger and bigger. Suddenly, Ben's jaw (drop) wide open. Five big black dragons (flies) outside his window.

The dragons (calls) to Benjamin. "Come fly with us!" they shout. Benjamin (think) about it. In a few seconds, he (decide). In a flash, he (jump) onto one of the dragons. The new friends (zooms) into the air. Benjamin laughs and (wonder) what will happen next.

Benjamin wakes at sunrise. He **looks** outside his apartment window. At

first, he **sees** only the sun. Then he **spots** five black dots in the distance.

The dots **grow** bigger and bigger. Suddenly, Ben's jaw **drops** wide open.

Five big black dragons **fly** outside his window.

The dragons **call** to Benjamin. "Come fly with us!" they shout.

Benjamin **thinks** about it. In a few seconds, he **decides**. In a flash, he

jumps onto one of the dragons. The new friends **zoom** into the air.

Benjamin laughs and **wonders** what will happen next.

Assessment Tip: Total **12** Points

Name _____

Planning Your Writing

Use this page to plan your opinion. Then number your reasons or details in the order you will use them.

Answers will vary.

Topic: <u>(2 points)</u>

Topic Sentence: <u>(2)</u>

Reason/Details: (2)

Reason/Details: (2)

Reason/Details: (2)

Reason/Details: (2)

Name _____

Using Commas with Introductory Phrases

Select the introductory group of words from the box that best completes each sentence.

> for example   first of all   in addition
>
> in conclusion   most important

Cats Are the Best Pets

    I think cats are the best pets. (1)

<u>First of all, **(1 point)**</u> they are fun to watch.

(2) <u>For example, **(1)**</u> if you roll a ball in front of it, a cat will bat it around the house.

(3) <u>In addition, **(1)**</u> cats like to play with string for hours. (4) <u>Most important, **(1)**</u> cats are good companions. They follow you around the house, and they sleep in your lap. (5) <u>In conclusion, **(1)**</u> those are the reasons why I think cats are the best pets!

Assessment Tip: Total **5** Points

Name _____

A Garden of Words

Circle the word that best completes each sentence.
Then write the word in the blank.

1. The elephants were so large they were __awesome **(1) point)**__ .
   A. impossible   C. (awesome) **(1)**
   B. weak   D. smart

2. My teacher __convinced **(1)**__ me that some kinds of plants can eat insects.
   A. discovered   C. rewarded
   B. disappeared   D. (convinced) **(1)**

3. I saw a bird in a tree, but it flew off and __disappeared **(1)**__ .
   A. (disappeared) **(1)**   C. grew
   B. discovered   D. walked

4. In the pond, I __discovered **(1)**__ a frog that looked like a leaf.
   A. thought   C. convinced
   B. (discovered) **(1)**   D. read

5. We thought the lion's loud roar was __incredible **(1)**__ .
   A. quiet   C. (incredible) **(1)**
   B. tiny   D. impossible

6. It was almost __impossible **(1)**__ to see the white polar bear sitting in the white snow.
   A. best   C. incredible
   B. awesome   D. (impossible) **(1)**

Name _____

Story Map

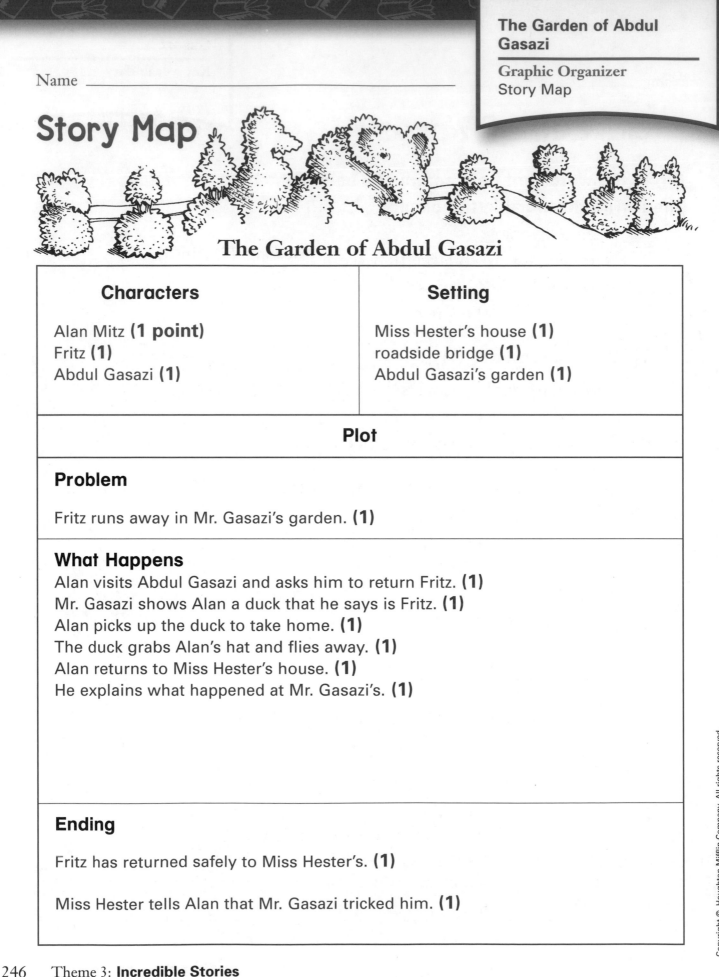

The Garden of Abdul Gasazi

Characters	Setting
Alan Mitz **(1 point)** Fritz **(1)** Abdul Gasazi **(1)**	Miss Hester's house **(1)** roadside bridge **(1)** Abdul Gasazi's garden **(1)**

Plot

Problem

Fritz runs away in Mr. Gasazi's garden. **(1)**

What Happens

Alan visits Abdul Gasazi and asks him to return Fritz. **(1)**

Mr. Gasazi shows Alan a duck that he says is Fritz. **(1)**

Alan picks up the duck to take home. **(1)**

The duck grabs Alan's hat and flies away. **(1)**

Alan returns to Miss Hester's house. **(1)**

He explains what happened at Mr. Gasazi's. **(1)**

Ending

Fritz has returned safely to Miss Hester's. **(1)**

Miss Hester tells Alan that Mr. Gasazi tricked him. **(1)**

Assessment Tip: Total **15** Points

Name _____

Mr. Gasazi's Garden!

Complete each sentence with an event from
The Garden of Abdul Gasazi. **Then explain how**
you feel about the way the story ends.

Sample answers are provided.

1. Miss Hester must visit Cousin Eunice, so she asks

   Alan Mitz to watch Fritz. **(1 point)**

2. When Alan takes Fritz for a walk,

   Fritz runs away in the Abdul Gasazi's garden. **(1)**

3. As Alan searches for Fritz, he finds Mr. Gasazi's home. **(1)**

4. The magician tells Alan that he has turned Fritz into a duck. **(1)**

5. As Alan leaves, the duck flies off with his hat. **(1)**

6. When Alan returns to Miss Hester's, Fritz is already there at

   the house. **(1)**

7. Miss Hester tells Alan that Mr. Gasazi played a trick on him. **(1)**

8. After Alan leaves, Miss Hester tells Fritz that he is a bad dog

   because he has Alan's hat. **(1)**

My Feelings About the Ending:

Answers will vary. **(2)**

_____

_____

Name _____

The Shape of a Story

Read the story below.

Rescuing Dolly

One cold morning as Keisha walked her dog, Vista, she noticed fresh tracks in the snow. A minute later, a small, spotted dog appeared by the river. With no tag or collar, it clearly was lost. It stared hopefully at Keisha and shivered in the cold. Then Vista barked, and the dog ran off. "It's much too cold for a dog to stay outside for long," Keisha thought. "I've got to do something, but Vista will keep scaring it away."

So Keisha headed for home. She told her mother about the lost dog, and together they returned to the river to find it.

Keisha was almost ready to give up, but at last she spotted the dog. Keisha called to it, but it jumped onto a rock. Then Keisha knelt down. The little dog leaped into her arms and began licking her face.

Weeks later, the little dog's owner still could not be found. So that is how Dolly, the little dog, came to be part of Keisha's family.

Name _____

The Shape of a Story continued

Fill in this story map with details from "Rescuing Dolly."

Characters	Setting
1. Keisha **(1 point)**	the snowy riverbank **(1)**
2. the lost dog **(1)**	

Plot

Problem

Keisha wants to save the lost dog. **(1)**

What Happens

1. She must take Vista home. **(1)**

2. She and her mother return to the river to look for it. **(1)**

3. She calls it, but the dog jumps onto a rock. **(1)**

4. Keisha kneels down. **(1)**

Ending

1. The dog jumps into Keisha's arms. **(1)**

2. Dolly, the dog, becomes part of Keisha's family. **(1)**

Name _____

Playing with Prefixes

On each line, write a word that begins with the prefix *un-, dis-,* or *non-* and matches the definition. Then find and circle all eight words in the word search.

1. not locked <u>unlocked</u> **(1 point)** _____

2. not fiction <u>nonfiction</u> **(1)** _____

3. the opposite of agree <u>disagree</u> **(1)** _____

4. not able <u>unable</u> **(1)** _____

5. the opposite of appear <u>disappear</u> **(1)** _____

6. not usual <u>unusual</u> **(1)** _____

7. not fair <u>unfair</u> **(1)** _____

8. not making sense <u>nonsense</u> **(1)** _____

```
K N O N F I C T I O N D A D F P E P
D E R W H Y N E Z G Q J X H G H T V
I Z W U C Q X U S Y C Y S S V M Z C
S T V A N L N O N S E N S E Z P G Z
A N P K A L M B S U I G I V K A O R
P V N O W J O O D G S P H Q M H M Z
P T G J G Z O C R S S U N F A I R
E R Y X W L P F K X M P A Z H Z A R
A H E R J Q M W M E G V T L M O J E
R E U N A B L E L P D I S A G R E E
```

(1 point per word in word search)

Assessment Tip: Total **16** Points

Name _____

Homophones

Homophones are words that sound the same but have different spellings and meanings. When you spell a homophone, think about the meaning of the word you want to write.

Homophone	**Meaning**
/nōō/ **new**	not old
/nōō/ **knew**	understood

Write the four pairs of Spelling Words that are homophones. Order of answers may vary.

hear **(1 point)**

here **(1)**

new **(1)**

knew **(1)**

its **(1)**

it's **(1)**

our **(1)**

hour **(1)**

Spelling Words

1. hear
2. here
3. new
4. knew
5. its
6. it's
7. our
8. hour
9. there
10. their
11. they're

Now write the three Spelling Words that are homophones. Order of answers may vary.

there **(1 point)**

their **(1)**

they're **(1)**

Assessment Tip: Total **11** Points

Name _____

Spelling Spree

Quotation Caper Write the Spelling Word that best completes each quotation that might have come from the story.

1. "We magicians never reveal _____ secrets," said Mr. Gasazi.

2. "Your hat is not in _____ usual place," said Miss Hester.

3. "The ducks have flown back to _____ pond," said Alan.

4. "Fritz, come back _____ !" called Alan.

5. "Dogs should know that _____ not welcome here," grumbled Gasazi.

1. our **(1 point)**   4. here **(1)**

2. its **(1)**   5. they're **(1)**

3. their **(1)**

In Another Word Write a Spelling Word to replace each expression.

6. get wind of   hear **(1)**

7. hot off the press new **(1)**

8. over yonder   there **(1)**

9. got the picture   knew **(1)**

Assessment Tip: Total **9** Points

Name _____

Proofreading and Writing

Proofreading Suppose that Alan keeps a journal. Circle the five misspelled Spelling Words in this entry. Then write each word correctly.

> **June 3:** Today I had a strange adventure. It was in a magician's garden. Miss Hester's dog Fritz ran in (their.) I (knue) we were in trouble when I read the sign: "No dogs allowed." I chased Fritz for at least an (our.) I think (its') possible that the magician turned Fritz into a duck! When I came back (heere,) no one believed my story.

<table>
<tr><td>Spelling Words</td></tr>
</table>

1. hear
2. here
3. new
4. knew
5. its
6. it's
7. our
8. hour
9. there
10. their
11. they're

1. there **(1 point)**
2. knew **(1)**
3. hour **(1)**
4. it's **(1)**
5. here **(1)**

Write a Plan Abdul Gasazi had some amazing trees in his garden. If you could plan a garden, what would you plant in it? Where would you plant things?

On a separate sheet of paper, draw a picture of your garden. Then write a plan for it. Tell what you would plant, and where. Use Spelling Words from the list. Responses will vary. **(5 points)**

Name _____

Ask Your Friendly Thesaurus!

For each underlined word in the following sentences, choose a better word or words from the thesaurus entry. Write your answers in the blanks provided. Some words may have more than one answer.

Thesaurus Entries

1. **funny:** silly, unusual, curious, laughable
2. **pulled:** strained, dragged, stretched, heaved
3. **ran:** darted, flowed, fled, hurried
4. **tired:** exhausted, faint, worn, wilting
5. **walking:** strolling, trotting, striding, stomping
6. **shouted:** called, bellowed, howled, bawled

1. Fritz stopped chewing the furniture and fell asleep,

   completely <u>tired</u>. word from item 4 **(1 point)** _____

2. Alan fastened Fritz's leash and the dog <u>pulled</u> him out of

   the house. word from item 2 **(1)** _____

3. Fritz <u>ran</u> straight through the open door.

   word from item 3 **(1)** _____

4. Gasazi <u>shouted</u> that he had turned the dogs into ducks!

   word from item 6 **(1)** _____

5. Alan felt <u>funny</u> when he thought the magician had fooled

   him. word from item 1 **(1)** _____

6. Fritz came <u>walking</u> up the front steps with Alan's hat.

   word from item 5 **(1)** _____

Assessment Tip: Total **6** Points

Name _____

Choosing Time

**Choose the correct verb form in parentheses and
write it on the line provided to complete the sentence.**

1. Tomorrow Alan <u>will take **(1)**</u>_____ Fritz for
   a walk. (takes   will take)

2. Yesterday Alan <u>searched **(1)**</u>_____ for Fritz.
   (searched   will search)

3. Yesterday in the garden, Fritz <u>bumped **(1)**</u>_____
   into Abdul. (bumped   will bump)

4. Tomorrow Alan <u>will climb **(1)**</u>_____ the stairs.
   (climbed   will climb)

5. Yesterday the ducks <u>flapped **(1)**</u>_____

   their wings. (flapped   will flap)

**Complete the chart by supplying past and
future time for each of the verbs given.**

Verb	Past Time	Future Time
try	tried **(1)**	will try **(1)**
race	raced **(1)**	will race **(1)**
disappear	disappeared **(1)**	will disappear **(1)**
drag	dragged **(1)**	will drag **(1)**
bolt	bolted **(1)**	will bolt **(1)**

Theme 3: **Incredible Stories**   255
Assessment Tip: Total **15** Points

Name _____

Writing Past and Future

Read each sentence. Then write the sentence in past time and future time.

1. Alan walks Fritz.

   Past: Alan walked Fritz. **(1 point)**

   Future: Alan will walk Fritz. **(1)**

2. He hurries after the dog.

   Past: He hurried after the dog. **(1)**

   Future: He will hurry after the dog. **(1)**

3. Alan discovers the magician.

   Past: Alan discovered the magician. **(1)**

   Future: Alan will discover the magician. **(1)**

4. Abdul shows Alan a duck.

   Past: Abdul showed Alan a duck. **(1)**

   Future: Abdul will show Alan a duck. **(1)**

5. The duck grabs Alan's hat.

   Past: The duck grabbed Alan's hat. **(1)**

   Future: The duck will grab Alan's hat. **(1)**

Assessment Tip: Total **10** Points

Name _____

Keeping Verbs Consistent

Read this story. The paragraphs mix up the past, the present, and the future. The story takes place in the past. Circle any verbs that are not in past time. Then write the verbs correctly on the lines below. Each verb is **1 point**.

I visited a strange garden yesterday. The bushes (look) like different animals. A giant green elephant (watches) the main path. I discovered a hidden path. I (will follow) the trail.

A strange noise (sounds) behind me. I turned around. The elephant (moves!) Then the giant plant (faces) in the other direction.

I (decide) to leave the weird garden. I (try) to find my way out. I looked everywhere. The paths twisted and turned.

I (turn) around again. The elephant (watches) me. I (step) farther into the garden. The elephant stared.

Finally, I (uncover) a hidden gate. I (hurry) toward it. The elephant (appears) in front of me. I raced out of the garden. Then I (glance) back. The garden (is) gone.

looked	moved	turned	hurried
watched	faced	watched	appeared
followed	decided	stepped	glanced
sounded	tried	uncovered	was

Assessment Tip: Total **16** Points

Name _____

Writing Dialogue

Write a dialogue, or a conversation between two or more
characters in a story. Try to make the dialogue sound as if
real people are talking. Use quotation marks in your dialogue.
Choose one of the following groups
of characters for your dialogue:

► Alan and Miss Hester
► Alan and Abdul Gasazi
► Miss Hester and Abdul Gasazi
► Alan, Miss Hester, and Abdul Gasazi
► Two characters from another story of your choice

Dialogues will vary. **(10 points)**

_____

_____

_____

_____

_____

_____

_____

_____

_____

_____

_____

_____

Assessment Tip: Total **10** Points

Name _____

Write Quotations Right!

Rewrite each of the following sentences of dialogue that might have taken place. Add quotation marks, capital letters, or commas.

1. Miss Hester said please stay with Fritz and give him his afternoon walk.

   Miss Hester said, "Please stay with Fritz and give him his afternoon walk." **(2 points)**

2. don't chew on the furniture, Fritz Alan said angrily.

   "Don't chew on the furniture, Fritz," Alan said angrily. **(2)**

3. please, Fritz Alan exclaimed don't go running off into that garden!

   "Please, Fritz," Alan exclaimed, "don't go running off into that garden!" **(2)**

4. Alan said if you have Fritz, Mr. Gasazi, would you please give him back?

   Alan said, "If you have Fritz, Mr. Gasazi, would you please give him back?" **(2)**

5. something terrible has happened, Miss Hester Alan blurted out. your dog ran away, and Mr. Gasazi turned him into a duck!

   "Something terrible has happened, Miss Hester," Alan blurted out. "Your dog ran away, and Mr. Gasazi turned him into a duck!" **(2)**

Theme 3: **Incredible Stories**   259
Assessment Tip: Total **10** Points

Name _____

Pig Escape Words!

Write each word next to its meaning.

1. to happily roll around in something <u>wallow</u> **(1 point)**

2. running away in fear <u>fleeing</u> **(1)**

3. a big adventure <u>escapade</u> **(1)**

4. a safe place for animals or people <u>sanctuary</u> **(1)**

Vocabulary

escapade
fleeing
sanctuary
wallow

Write sentences to answer these questions.
Answers will vary. Sample answers are given.

5. Why is a sanctuary an important place for some animals?

   <u>Sample answer: It keeps them safe from other animals that might hurt them.</u> **(1)**

6. If you went on an escapade, what do you think you might do?

   <u>Sample answer: I would try to visit a place where I had never been before.</u> **(1)**

7. What could happen to make an animal start fleeing?

   <u>Sample answer: It might hear a loud noise.</u> **(1)**

8. What do pigs like to wallow in?

   <u>Sample answer: They like to wallow in mud.</u> **(1)**

Assessment Tip: Total **8** Points

Name _____

Fantasy or Reality?

As you read the stories, write down the incredible things that happen. If an event happened in real life, write an R next to it. If the event is fantasy, write an F.

Answers will vary, but should reflect that the events in *Fugitives on Four Legs* are real life and that those in *Dinosaur Bob* are make-believe. Sample answers are given.

Story	What incredible things happen?	Real life or fantasy?
Fugitives on Four Legs	1. Two pigs escape and run free for over a week. **(1 point)** 2. The pigs become famous. **(1)** 3. Someone pays a lot of money for the pigs. **(1)**	1. R **(1)** 2. R **(1)** 3. R **(1)**
Dinosaur Bob	1. The Lazardos find a dinosaur and call him Bob. **(1)** 2. The Lazardos sail down the Nile on Bob's back. **(1)** 3. Bob sleeps in an ocean liner's smokestack. **(1)**	1. F **(1)** 2. F **(1)** 3. F **(1)**

Assessment Tip: Total **12** Points

The Boar Facts

Think about the selection. Then complete the sentences.
Exact wording of some answers may vary.

1. The names of the pigs that escaped were Butch and Sundance **(2 points)**.

2. The place where this happened was Malmesbury, England **(2)**.

3. The amount of time the pigs ran free was over a week **(2)**.

4. The pigs' adventures made the news in Europe and the United States **(2)**.

5. Today, the pigs live in an animal sanctuary **(2)**.

Theme 3: **Incredible Stories**   263
Assessment Tip: Total **10** Points

Travel Words

Fill each blank with the Key Vocabulary word that best completes the sentence.

Do you need a vacation? We can find the perfect trip for you!

Would you like to visit Africa? Let us send you on a safari **(2 points)**. You'll see lions, giraffes, and gazelles. Be careful, though. Lions can be a menace **(2)** if you wander alone.

Maybe you'd like a Western vacation instead. You can learn to ride a horse and sleep under the stars. Around the campfire, you'll be honored with a singing cowboy serenade **(2)**. Our real-life cowhands will give you a rendition **(2)** of "Home on the Range."

How would you like to sail on a big ocean liner **(2)**? On the ship you'll stay in a cozy berth **(2)**, with a bed and a window. Let us take you wherever you want to go!

Assessment Tip: Total **12** Points

Name _____

Test Practice

Use the three steps you've learned to write a personal response to these questions about *Dinosaur Bob*. Make a chart on a separate piece of paper, and then write your response on the lines below. Use the checklist to revise your response.

1. Suppose Dinosaur Bob went on a trip with your family. What might happen? Include many details.

Use the checklist to score each student's response.

_____

_____

_____

_____

_____

_____

_____

_____

Personal Response Checklist

✔ Did I restate the question at the beginning? **(2 points)**

✔ Can I add more details from what I read to support my answer? **(5)**

✔ Can I add more of my experiences to support my answer? **(5)**

✔ Do I need to delete any details that do not help answer the question? **(2)**

✔ Did I use clear handwriting? Did I make any mistakes? **(4)**

Continue on page 266.

Test Practice continued

2. **Connecting/Comparing** Suppose you could choose either Dinosaur Bob or the dragon in *Raising Dragons* to be your pet. Explain which one you would choose and why.

Use the checklist to score each student's response.

_____

_____

_____

_____

_____

_____

_____

_____

_____

_____

Personal Response Checklist

✔ Did I restate the question at the beginning? **(2 points)**

✔ Can I add more details from what I read to support my answer? **(5)**

✔ Can I add more of my experiences to support my answer? **(5)**

✔ Do I need to delete any details that do not help answer the question? **(2)**

✔ Did I use clear handwriting? Did I make any mistakes? **(4)**

Read your answers to Questions I and 2 aloud to a partner. Then discuss the checklist. Make any changes that will make your answers better.

Assessment Tip: Total **36** Points

Name _____

Action Plan

Read the paragraph. Then list the steps on the lines below.

Paper Hearts

Materials: construction paper, pencil, scissors

Directions: First fold the paper in half. Next draw half of a heart shape with the straight side on the edge with the fold. Then cut along the outline. Finally, open the folded paper.

Steps:

1. Fold the paper in half. **(1 point)**

2. Draw half a heart shape with the straight side on the edge with the fold. **(1)**

3. Cut along the outline. **(1)**

4. Open the folded paper. **(1)**

What materials should you gather before beginning the project?

construction paper, pencil, scissors **(3)**

Why is it important to follow each step in order?

Answers will vary. Sample response: If you don't follow the

steps in order, the paper heart will not come out right. **(3)**

Name _____

The Shape of a Story

Read the story elements listed below from *The Mysterious Giant of Barletta*. Then write the number for each element on the correct line below. More than one number may go on some lines.

1. An army is coming to destroy the peaceful town of Barletta.
2. Zia Concetta
3. The giant uses an onion to trick the army into leaving the town alone.
4. The peace and quiet disappear as everyone becomes fearful of the army's arrival.
5. the Mysterious Giant
6. a lieutenant
7. Zia asks the giant for assistance and he agrees to help.
8. The giant grabs a large onion and goes to meet the army.
9. Captain Minckion
10. the town of Barletta

Who are the characters in this story? 2, 5, 6, 9 **(4 points)**

Where does the story take place? 10 **(1)**

What is the story problem? 1 **(1)**

What happens before the problem is solved? 4, 7, 8 **(3)**

What happens to solve the problem? 3 **(1)**

268   Theme 3: **Incredible Stories**
Assessment Tip: Total **10** Points

Name _____

What's This Word?

Read the information in the chart. Then unscramble each word below, using what you know about the five prefixes listed in the chart and the clues in parentheses.

Prefix	Meaning	Example
un-	"not" or "the opposite of"	untrue
dis-	"not" or "the opposite of"	disappear
non-	"not" or "the opposite of"	nonfiction
bi-	"two"	bicycle
mis-	"wrong"	misbehave

1. **EIEARGSD**   (fail to agree) disagree **(1 point)**

2. **DIUETN**   (not tied) untied **(1)**

3. **SSMUEI**   (use wrongly) misuse **(1)**

4. **YEKLIBEW**   (every two weeks) biweekly **(1)**

5. **RDSTUIST**   (opposite of *trust*) distrust **(1)**

6. **PUPDIZEN**   (opposite of *zipped*) unzipped **(1)**

7. **OSPONTN**   (without stops) nonstop **(1)**

8. **SLIPSLEM**   (spell in a way that is not correct) misspell **(1)**

9. **ENABILP**   (plane with double wings) biplane **(1)**

10. **PYNUAPH**   (not happy) unhappy **(1)**

Assessment Tip: Total **10** Points

Name _____

Choose the Correct Meaning

Read the definitions in the dictionary entries below.

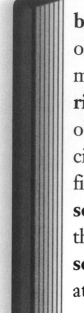

bank (băngk) *noun* **1.** Ground, often sloping, along the edge of a river, creek, or pond. **2.** Sideways tilt of an airplane when making a turn. **3.** Place or container where money is kept.
ring (rĭng) *noun* **1.** The sound made by a bell or other metallic object. **2.** Any loud sound that is continued or repeated. **3.** A circle with an empty center. **4.** A small circular band worn on a finger.
scan (skăn) *verb* **1.** To examine something closely or thoroughly. **2.** To look something over quickly.
scout (skout) *verb* **1.** To explore a place. **2.** To observe an athlete for possible hiring by a sports team.

Read each sentence below. Choose the correct meaning from the dictionary entries above for each underlined word. Write the number of the correct meaning on the line provided.

1. We camped inside a <u>ring</u> of pine trees. 3 **(2 points)** _____

2. We waded between the steep <u>banks</u>. 1 **(2)** _____

3. He <u>scouted</u> a way to the top of the hill. 1 **(2)** _____

4. Looking up for a moment, she <u>scanned</u> the trail ahead.

   2 **(2)** _____

5. The pilot put the glider into a severe <u>bank</u> to change course.

   2 **(2)** _____

Assessment Tip: Total **10** Points

Name _____

Spelling Review

**Write each Spelling Word. Then circle six words that
are homophone pairs.** Order of answers may vary.

1. word **(1 point)**
2. sound **(1)**
3. clear **(1)**
4. also **(1)**
5. soft **(1)**
6. crack **(1)**
7. lawn **(1)**
8. crown **(1)**
9. girl **(1)**
10. (knew) **(1) / (1)**
11. (here) **(1) / (1)**
12. turn **(1)**

13. dark **(1)**
14. north **(1)**
15. orange **(1)**
16. her **(1)**
17. skin **(1)**
18. (hear) **(1) / (1)**
19. squeeze **(1)**
20. gym **(1)**
21. second **(1)**
22. jeans **(1)**
23. (hour) **(1) / (1)**
24. (our) **(1) / (1)**
25. (new) **(1) / (1)**

Spelling Words

1. word
2. sound
3. clear
4. also
5. soft
6. crack
7. lawn
8. crown
9. girl
10. knew
11. here
12. turn
13. dark
14. north
15. orange
16. her
17. skin
18. hear
19. squeeze
20. gym
21. second
22. jeans
23. hour
24. our
25. new

Assessment Tip: Total **31** Points

Name _____

Spelling Spree

Puzzle Play Write a Spelling Word for each clue.
Then use the letters in the boxes to spell a word
about what a dragon is like.

1. sound
2. lawn
3. crown
4. girl
5. skin
6. crack
7. gym
8. orange
9. second
10. jeans
11. hear
12. hour

1. this covers your body   s k i n   **(1)**

2. first, —, third   s e c o n d   **(1)**

3. heavy blue pants   j e a n s   **(1)**

4. 60 minutes   h o u r   **(1)**

5. a large indoor play area   g y m   **(1)**

Secret Word: scary _____

Picture Clues Write Spelling
Words for each sentence.

6–7.   The girl **(1)** _____ is holding an

orange **(1)** _____ .

8–9.   Stones from the crack **(1)** _____ in

the wall are lying on the lawn **(1)** _____ .

10–12. The king, wearing his crown **(1)** _____ ,

cannot hear **(1)** _____ the soft

sound **(1)** _____ .

Assessment Tip: Total **12** Points

Name _____

Proofreading and Writing

Proofreading Circle the five misspelled Spelling
Words below. Write each word correctly.

It can be lonely (hear) in my big house. I don't
hear a (werd) from morning until (darc). This morning,
however, I heard a (saft) sound. It was my friend
Masha, who held out a hand for me to (skweeze.)

1. here **(1 point)** _____   4. soft **(1)** _____

2. word **(1)** _____   5. squeeze **(1)** _____

3. dark **(1)** _____

Spelling Words

1. clear
2. girl
3. turn
4. also
5. squeeze
6. dark
7. soft
8. north
9. her
10. new
11. here
12. our
13. knew
14. word

Which Word? Write the Spelling Word that best fits
each group of words.

6. understood or   knew **(1)**   11. opposite of south   north **(1)**

7. unused or   new **(1)**   12. boy and   girl **(1)**

8. in addition   also **(1)**   13. to spin, circle, or   turn **(1)**

9. sunny and   clear **(1)**   14. we, us,   our **(1)**

10. his or her   her **(1)**

Write Directions On another sheet of paper, write
directions telling the giant how to get from your
school to your house. Use the Spelling Review
Words. Responses will vary. **(6)**

Name _____

Writing Possessives

**On the line provided, write the correct possessive form of
the noun in parentheses to complete each sentence. Then
write *S* if the possessive noun is singular and *P* if it is
plural.**

1. The pigs' **(2 points)**_____ escapade began on market day in

   Malmesbury, England. (pigs) P_____

2. They spoiled a butcher's **(2)**_____ plan by escaping from

   him. (butcher) S_____

3. The two pigs trotted through farmers' **(2)**_____ fields.

   (farmers) P_____

4. They rooted around in families' **(2)**_____ gardens.

   (families) P_____

5. These plump animals avoided a policeman's **(2)**_____ net.

   (policeman) S_____

6. They became the country's **(2)**_____ favorite pigs.

   (country) S_____

Assessment Tip: Total **12** Points

Writing Past and Future

**Read each sentence. Then write the sentence in past time
and future time.**

1. Scotty returns with a dinosaur.

    Past: Scotty returned with a dinosaur. **(1 point)**

    Future: Scotty will return with a dinosaur. **(1)**

2. Bob carries the family down the river.

    Past: Bob carried the family down the river. **(1)**

    Future: Bob will carry the family down the river. **(1)**

3. Zelda plays baseball with the others.

    Past: Zelda played baseball with the others. **(1)**

    Future: Zelda will play baseball with the others. **(1)**

4. The family sails on a big ship.

    Past: The family sailed on a big ship. **(1)**

    Future: The family will sail on a big ship. **(1)**

5. Passengers dance on Bob's back.

    Past: Passengers danced on Bob's back. **(1)**

    Future: Passengers will dance on Bob's back. **(1)**

Theme 3: **Incredible Stories**   275
Assessment Tip: Total **10** Points

Student Handbook

Contents

Spelling

How to Study a Word   **279**

Words Often Misspelled   **280**

Take-Home Word Lists   **281**

Grammar and Usage

Problem Words   **295**

Proofreading Checklist   **296**

Proofreading Marks   **297**

How to Study a Word

1. LOOK at the word.
▶ What does the word mean?
▶ What letters are in the word?
▶ Name and touch each letter.

2. SAY the word.
▶ Listen for the consonant sounds.
▶ Listen for the vowel sounds.

3. THINK about the word.
▶ How is each sound spelled?
▶ Close your eyes and picture the word.
▶ What familiar spelling patterns do you see?
▶ What other words have the same spelling patterns?

4. WRITE the word.
▶ Think about the sounds and the letters.
▶ Form the letters correctly.

5. CHECK the spelling.
▶ Did you spell the word the same way it is spelled in your word list?
▶ If you did not spell the word correctly, write the word again.

about	don't	I'd		
again	down	I'll		
almost		I'm	outside	tonight
a lot	enough	into		too
also	every	its	people	two
always	everybody	it's	pretty	
am				until
and	family	January	really	
another	favorite		right	very
anyone	February	knew		
anyway	field	know	said	want
around	finally		Saturday	was
	for	letter	school	Wednesday
beautiful	found	like	some	we're
because	friend	little	something	where
been	from	lose	started	while
before		lying	stopped	who
brought	getting		sure	whole
buy	girl	might	swimming	world
	goes	morning		would
cannot	going	mother	than	wouldn't
can't	guess	myself	that's	write
clothes			their	writing
coming	happily	never	them	
could	have	new	then	you
cousin	haven't	now	there	your
	heard		they	
does	her	off	thought	
didn't	here	one	through	
different	his	other	to	
done	how	our	today	

The Ballad of Mulan

More Short Vowels
/ŏ/ ➤ lot
/ŭ/ ➤ rub

Spelling Words
1. pond
2. luck
3. drop
4. lot
5. rub
6. does
7. drum
8. sock
9. hunt
10. crop
11. shut
12. won

Challenge Words
1. dodge
2. dusk

My Study List
Add your own spelling words on the back. ➤

Off to Adventure!
Reading-Writing Workshop

Look for familiar spelling patterns in these words to help you remember their spellings.

Spelling Words
1. have
2. haven't
3. found
4. around
5. one
6. than
7. then
8. them
9. before
10. because
11. other
12. mother

Challenge Words
1. family
2. cousin
3. everybody
4. guess

My Study List
Add your own spelling words on the back. ➤

Cliff Hanger

Short Vowels
/ă/ ➤ last
/ĕ/ ➤ smell
/ĭ/ ➤ mix

Spelling Words
1. mix
2. milk
3. smell
4. last
5. head
6. friend
7. class
8. left
9. thick
10. send
11. thin
12. stick

Challenge Words
1. empty
2. glance

My Study List
Add your own spelling words on the back. ➤

Name _____

1. _____
2. _____
3. _____
4. _____
5. _____
6. _____
7. _____
8. _____
9. _____
10. _____

Review Words

1. test
2. dish

How to Study a Word

Look at the word.
Say the word.
Think about the word.
Write the word.
Check the spelling.

282

Name _____

1. _____
2. _____
3. _____
4. _____
5. _____
6. _____
7. _____
8. _____
9. _____
10. _____

How to Study a Word

Look at the word.
Say the word.
Think about the word.
Write the word.
Check the spelling.

282

Name _____

1. _____
2. _____
3. _____
4. _____
5. _____
6. _____
7. _____
8. _____
9. _____
10. _____

Review Words

1. hop
2. much

How to Study a Word

Look at the word.
Say the word.
Think about the word.
Write the word.
Check the spelling.

282

The Keeping Quilt

More Long Vowel Spellings

/ā/ → p**ai**nt, cl**ay**

/ē/ → l**ea**ve, f**ee**l

Spelling Words

1. paint
2. clay
3. feel
4. leave
5. neighbor
6. eight
7. seem
8. speak
9. paid
10. lay
11. need
12. weigh

Challenge Words

1. needle
2. crayon

My Study List
Add your own spelling words on the back. ➡

Off to Adventure!
Spelling Review

Spelling Words

1. last
2. mix
3. stick
4. lot
5. sock
6. hunt
7. wide
8. grade
9. thick
10. send
11. class
12. pond
13. luck
14. drum
15. save
16. cube
17. smile
18. left
19. smell
20. thin
21. drop
22. shut
23. huge
24. note
25. life

See the back for Challenge Words.

My Study List
Add your own spelling words on the back. ➡

The Lost and Found

The Vowel-Consonant-*e* Pattern

/ā/ → s**a**v**e**

/ī/ → l**i**f**e**

/ō/ → sm**o**k**e**

/yōō/ → h**u**g**e**

Spelling Words

1. smoke
2. huge
3. save
4. life
5. wide
6. come
7. mine
8. grade
9. smile
10. note
11. cube
12. love

Challenge Words

1. escape
2. slope

My Study List
Add your own spelling words on the back. ➡

Name _____

My Study List

1. _____
2. _____
3. _____
4. _____
5. _____
6. _____
7. _____
8. _____
9. _____
10. _____

Review Words

1. test
2. dish

How to Study a Word

Look at the word.
Say the word.
Think about the word.
Write the word.
Check the spelling.

284

Name _____

My Study List

1. _____
2. _____
3. _____
4. _____
5. _____
6. _____
7. _____
8. _____
9. _____
10. _____

Challenge Words

1. glance
2. empty
3. dusk
4. slope
5. escape

How to Study a Word

Look at the word.
Say the word.
Think about the word.
Write the word.
Check the spelling.

284

Name _____

My Study List

1. _____
2. _____
3. _____
4. _____
5. _____
6. _____
7. _____
8. _____
9. _____
10. _____

Review Words

1. clean
2. play

How to Study a Word

Look at the word.
Say the word.
Think about the word.
Write the word.
Check the spelling.

284

The Talking Cloth

Three-Letter Clusters and Unexpected Consonant Patterns
spring
street
throw

/n/	➡	**kn**ee
/r/	➡	**wr**ap
/ch/	➡	wa**tch**

Spelling Words

1. spring	7. three
2. knee	8. watch
3. throw	9. street
4. patch	10. know
5. strong	11. spread
6. wrap	12. write

Challenge Words
1. strength
2. kitchen

My Study List
Add your own spelling words on the back. ➡

Grandma's Records

The Long *o* Sound
/ō/ ➡ c**oa**ch, bl**ow**, h**o**ld

Spelling Words

1. coach
2. blow
3. float
4. hold
5. sew
6. though
7. sold
8. soap
9. row
10. own
11. both
12. most

Challenge Words
1. tomorrow
2. program

My Study List
Add your own spelling words on the back. ➡

Celebrating Traditions
Reading-Writing Workshop

Look for familiar spelling patterns in these words to help you remember their spellings.

Spelling Words

1. now	7. cannot
2. off	8. about
3. for	9. always
4. almost	10. today
5. also	11. until
6. can't	12. again

Challenge Words
1. February
2. January
3. Saturday
4. Wednesday

My Study List
Add your own spelling words on the back. ➡

Take-Home Word List

Name _____

My Study List

1. _____
2. _____
3. _____
4. _____
5. _____
6. _____
7. _____
8. _____
9. _____
10. _____

How to Study a Word

Look at the word.
Say the word.
Think about the word.
Write the word.
Check the spelling.

Take-Home Word List

Name _____

My Study List

1. _____
2. _____
3. _____
4. _____
5. _____
6. _____
7. _____
8. _____
9. _____
10. _____

Review Words

1. cold
2. slow

How to Study a Word

Look at the word.
Say the word.
Think about the word.
Write the word.
Check the spelling.

Take-Home Word List

Name _____

My Study List

1. _____
2. _____
3. _____
4. _____
5. _____
6. _____
7. _____
8. _____
9. _____
10. _____

Review Words

1. catch
2. two

How to Study a Word

Look at the word.
Say the word.
Think about the word.
Write the word.
Check the spelling.

Dogzilla

The Vowel Sounds in *clown* and *lawn*

/ou/ → cl**ow**n, s**ou**nd

/ô/ → l**aw**n, cl**o**th, t**a**lk

Spelling Words

1. clown
2. lawn
3. talk
4. sound
5. cloth
6. would
7. also
8. mouth
9. crown
10. soft
11. count
12. law

Challenge Words

1. bounce
2. officer

My Study List
Add your own spelling words on the back. →

Celebrating Traditions
Spelling Review

Spelling Words

1. speak
2. feel
3. seem
4. most
5. both
6. know
7. street
8. lie
9. need
10. paint
11. hold
12. float
13. three
14. spread
15. mind
16. might
17. lay
18. leave
19. own
20. row
21. wrap
22. patch
23. tie
24. wild
25. bright

See the back for Challenge Words.

My Study List
Add your own spelling words on the back. →

Dancing Rainbows

The Long *i* Sound

/ī/ → br**igh**t, w**i**ld, d**ie**

Spelling Words

1. wild
2. bright
3. die
4. sight
5. child
6. pie
7. fight
8. lie
9. tight
10. tie
11. might
12. mind

Challenge Words

1. design
2. delight

My Study List
Add your own spelling words on the back. →

Name _____

My Study List

1. _____
2. _____
3. _____
4. _____
5. _____
6. _____
7. _____
8. _____
9. _____
10. _____

Review Words

1. find
2. high

How to Study a Word

Look at the word.
Say the word.
Think about the word.
Write the word.
Check the spelling.

Name _____

My Study List

1. _____
2. _____
3. _____
4. _____
5. _____
6. _____
7. _____
8. _____
9. _____
10. _____

Challenge Words

1. needle
2. tomorrow
3. program
4. kitchen
5. design

How to Study a Word

Look at the word.
Say the word.
Think about the word.
Write the word.
Check the spelling.

Name _____

My Study List

1. _____
2. _____
3. _____
4. _____
5. _____
6. _____
7. _____
8. _____
9. _____
10. _____

Review Words

1. town
2. small

How to Study a Word

Look at the word.
Say the word.
Think about the word.
Write the word.
Check the spelling.

Raising Dragons

The /j/, /k/, and /kw/ Sounds
/j/ ➜ jeans, large, gym
/k/ ➜ park, quick, picnic
/kw/ ➜ quick

Spelling Words

1. large
2. gym
3. skin
4. quick
5. picnic
6. judge
7. park
8. jeans
9. crack
10. orange
11. second
12. squeeze

Challenge Words

1. courage
2. insect

My Study List
Add your own spelling words on the back. ➜

The Mysterious Giant of Barletta

Vowel + /r/ Sounds
/är/ ➜ dark
/î\r/ ➜ clear
/ôr/ ➜ north
/ûr/ ➜ her, girl, turn, work

Spelling Words

1. girl
2. clear
3. her
4. turn
5. dark
6. work
7. smart
8. word
9. hurt
10. serve
11. north
12. third

Challenge Words

1. tornado
2. scurried

My Study List
Add your own spelling words on the back. ➜

Incredible Stories
Reading-Writing Workshop

Look for familiar spelling patterns in these words to help you remember their spellings.

Spelling Words

1. and
2. said
3. goes
4. going
5. some
6. something
7. you
8. your
9. friend
10. school
11. where
12. myself

Challenge Words

1. tonight
2. lying
3. field
4. enough

My Study List
Add your own spelling words on the back. ➜

Name _____

My Study List

1. _____
2. _____
3. _____
4. _____
5. _____
6. _____
7. _____
8. _____
9. _____
10. _____

How to Study a Word

Look at the word.
Say the word.
Think about the word.
Write the word.
Check the spelling.

Name _____

My Study List

1. _____
2. _____
3. _____
4. _____
5. _____
6. _____
7. _____
8. _____
9. _____
10. _____

Review Words

1. hard
2. morning

How to Study a Word

Look at the word.
Say the word.
Think about the word.
Write the word.
Check the spelling.

Name _____

My Study List

1. _____
2. _____
3. _____
4. _____
5. _____
6. _____
7. _____
8. _____
9. _____
10. _____

Review Words

1. rock
2. job

How to Study a Word

Look at the word.
Say the word.
Think about the word.
Write the word.
Check the spelling.

Incredible Stories
Spelling Review

Spelling Words

1. sound	14. second
2. crown	15. here
3. word	16. new
4. her	17. soft
5. crack	18. turn
6. orange	19. north
7. hear	20. skin
8. our	21. gym
9. also	22. jeans
10. girl	23. hour
11. dark	24. knew
12. clear	25. lawn
13. squeeze	

**See the back for
Challenge Words**

My Study List
Add your own
spelling words
on the back. ➡

The Garden of
Abdul Gasazi

Homophones
Homophones are
words that sound alike
but have different
spellings and
meanings.

Spelling Words

1. hear
2. here
3. new
4. knew
5. its
6. it's
7. our
8. hour
9. there
10. their
11. they're

Challenge Words

1. seen
2. scene

My Study List
Add your own
spelling words
on the back. ➡

Name _____

My Study List

1. _____
2. _____
3. _____
4. _____
5. _____
6. _____
7. _____
8. _____
9. _____
10. _____

Review Words

1. eye
2. I

How to Study a Word

Look at the word.
Say the word.
Think about the word.
Write the word.
Check the spelling.

292

Take-Home Word List

Name _____

My Study List

1. _____
2. _____
3. _____
4. _____
5. _____
6. _____
7. _____
8. _____
9. _____
10. _____

Challenge Words

1. officer
2. scurried
3. insect
4. seen
5. scene

How to Study a Word

Look at the word.
Say the word.
Think about the word.
Write the word.
Check the spelling.

292

Focus on Trickster Tales

The Vowel Sound in *join*

/oi/ ➤ j**oi**n, j**oy**

Spelling Words

1. join
2. joy
3. boil
4. noise
5. spoil
6. choice
7. soil
8. point
9. foil
10. voice
11. coil
12. broil

Challenge Words

1. enjoy
2. rejoice

My Study List
Add your own spelling words on the back. ➤

Focus on Poetry

More Short and Long Vowels

short vowel sounds ➤ st**a**nd, r**e**st, tw**i**st, cl**o**ck, st**u**ff

long vowel sounds ➤ pl**ate**, wh**ite**, sp**oke**, J**u**ne

Spelling Words

1. stand
2. rest
3. plate
4. clock
5. white
6. stuff
7. spoke
8. bend
9. frame
10. twist
11. June
12. mile

Challenge Words

1. liquid
2. decide

My Study List
Add your own spelling words on the back. ➤

Name _____

My Study List

1. _____
2. _____
3. _____
4. _____
5. _____
6. _____
7. _____
8. _____
9. _____
10. _____

Review Words

1. when
2. back

How to Study a Word

Look at the word.
Say the word.
Think about the word.
Write the word.
Check the spelling.

294

Name _____

My Study List

1. _____
2. _____
3. _____
4. _____
5. _____
6. _____
7. _____
8. _____
9. _____
10. _____

Review Words

1. coin
2. boy

How to Study a Word

Look at the word.
Say the word.
Think about the word.
Write the word.
Check the spelling.

294

Problem Words

Words	Rules	Examples
are our	*Are* is a verb. *Our* is a possessive pronoun.	<u>Are</u> these gloves yours? This is <u>our</u> car.
doesn't don't	Use *doesn't* with singular nouns, *he*, *she*, and *it*. Use *don't* with plural nouns, *I*, *you*, *we*, and *they*.	Dad <u>doesn't</u> swim. We <u>don't</u> swim.
good well	Use the adjective *good* to describe nouns. Use the adverb *well* to describe verbs.	The weather looks <u>good</u>. She sings <u>well</u>.
its it's	*Its* is a possessive pronoun. *It's* means "it is" (contraction).	The dog wagged <u>its</u> tail. <u>It's</u> cold today.
let leave	*Let* means "to allow." *Leave* means "to go away from" or "to let stay."	Please <u>let</u> me go swimming. I will <u>leave</u> soon. <u>Leave</u> it on my desk.
set sit	*Set* means "to put." *Sit* means "to rest or stay in one place."	<u>Set</u> the vase on the table. Please <u>sit</u> in this chair.
their there they're	*Their* means "belonging to them." *There* means "at or in that place." *They're* means "they are" (contraction).	<u>Their</u> coats are on the bed. Is Carlos <u>there</u>? <u>They're</u> going to the store.
two to too	*Two* is a number *To* means "toward." *Too* means "also" or "more than enough.	I bought <u>two</u> shirts. A cat ran <u>to</u> the tree. Can we go <u>too</u>? I ate <u>too</u> many peas.
your you're	*Your* is a possessive pronoun. *You're* means "you are" (contraction).	Are these <u>your</u> glasses? <u>You're</u> late again!

Proofreading
Checklist

Read each question below. Then check your paper. Correct any mistakes you find. After you have corrected them, put a check mark in the box next to the question.

☐   1. Did I indent each paragraph?

☐   2. Does each sentence tell one complete thought?

☐   3. Did I end each sentence with the correct end mark?

☐   4. Did I begin each sentence with a capital letter?

☐   5. Did I use capital letters correctly in other places?

☐   6. Did I use commas correctly?

☐   7. Did I spell all the words the right way?

Are there other problem areas you should watch for? Make your own proofreading checklist.

☐ _____

☐ _____

☐ _____

☐ _____

☐ _____

☐ _____

☐ _____

296   **Student Handbook**

Copyright © Houghton Mifflin Company. All rights reserved.

Proofreading Marks

Mark	Explanation	Examples
¶	Begin a new paragraph. Indent the paragraph.	¶The boat finally arrived. It was two hours late.
∧	Add letters, words, or sentences.	My friend ate lunch with me t^o day. best
℘	Take out words, sentences, and punctuation marks. Correct spelling.	We ~~looked at and~~ admired the moddel airplanes.
≡	Change a small letter to a capital letter.	New York city is exciting.
/	Change a capital letter to a small letter.	The Fireflies blinked in the dark.
ʽʽ ʼʼ	Add quotation marks.	Where do you want the piano? asked the movers.
∧	Add a comma.	Carlton my cat has a mind of his own.
⊙	Add a period.	Put a period at the end of the sentence.
∼	Reverse letters or words.	Raed carefully the instructions.
?	Add a question mark.	Should I put the mark here?
!	Add an exclamation mark.	Look out below!

Student Handbook